# *Sensing* Mr. Right Guy

## The Ultimate and Humorous Dating Guide for Women

by

Leagan E. Kasper

Korifaeus Publishing
New York City
©July 2015

Dear Reader

You may notice that i exclusively use the small letter i when referring to myself, instead of the capital I . It's not a typo - i do it in all of my writings, i.e., articles and books,  on purpose; because there's no rational reason to me why one should refer to oneself using a capital letter I, which looks so imposing, arrogant and pompous. The small i, however, looks modest, as well as cute with that little dot on top. In no other language than the english language is a capital first letter used to refer to oneself, while, when addressing someone, a capital first letter is used to show ' respect'.

Thus please excuse my use of the small letter i when referring to myself - or characters referring to themselves - i've grown fond of that little i because i can't take myself that serious, referring to myself using a capital letter.

# Chapters

## Preface

Like every woman in the world magnetically attracted to a certain type of man, he gets my attention the moment i spot him; i take a glance, sometimes just to delight in his appearance, his look.

Other times to give him a Cat-scan, closely observing his features, demeanor and attitude allowing a glimpse into his personality. It's entertaining because the more one is able to observe about a person, the more an entire picture of the person unfolds, which either leads me to grin, to chuckle or become more curious as to what he's all about.

It's much like being appetized  seeing a piece of cake in a supermarket, with no intention to look for a cake, rather to buy some cheese. Walking through the bakery isle to get to the cheese section, a chocolate butter-creme cake inadvertently catches my eye sight, and yummo, delicious.
Could it be real butter creme ?

I forget all about the cheese, because the cake seems so much more tempting than a piece of cheese at that moment. I would buy the entire cake, but i need to assure myself that it's real butter creme and tastes at least as good as it looks, even though the lady behind the counter assures me it's butter creme - they always do, but from past experiences i know it isn't  always the case - thus i purchase a small piece of that cake.

Finally home, the piece of cake on a plate in front of me, i could devour it in one swoop, but..... what if it's not real butter creme, instead some hydrogenated vegetable oil whipped up to look like creme, with brownish color added to give it the appearance of chocolate ?

Then i'll be burping from the stomach acid, end up with heart burn and…. regret not having used my senses and was fooled by the mere look of the cake.

To avoid regrets i thus take a good whiff of the cake and i can clearly smell some of the ingredients, making me mouth water. Chocolate - a touch of vanilla - and ooh what's that, roasted hazelnuts. It doesn't smell synthetic for sure and grab the fork, take a small piece of cake, allowing it to melt on my tongue, delighting in the aroma - the smell exuding from the hazelnuts when breathing out through my nose.

It's real butter creme alright, and i won't regret eating the piece of cake, savoring each bite.

That's how to go about dating ; if allured by the look and overall appearance of a man, take a whiff and see if the aroma entices or repels you. Using all of one's senses when first meeting a potential Mister Right Guy provides you with a 99.9 % chance of no regrets. I prefer to use all 7 senses, but if you want to use only 5 that's okay, too. The 7 senses are:
1. Sight
2. Hearing
3. Smell
4. Taste
5.Touch
6. Instinct/Gut
7. Imagination

# The Essence of a Scent

Once we notice a type of man, with that certain type of look - say at a coffee place - we first try to find out if he's married. Thus, innovative as we women are, we pretend to get some sugar at the counter where the possible Mr. Right-Guy just so happens to be standing, and grab a sugar package EVEN though we NEVER use sugar in our coffee.

And though we just want to get a glimpse of his left hand to check if he's wearing a wedding band, jolly gee, he smiles and oh la la, nice smile, suave, not imposing, just a pleasant non-pick-up artist smile. " He noticed me, how nice," is the inner thought - and getting a glimpse of his left hand, he's not wearing a wedding band.

That doesn't mean much, however, 'cuz not every married man wears a wedding band. But he smiled, thus let's accidentally drop the sugar right in front of his feet, which of course happened by mere accident; we instantly pick it up, he looks and the opportunity to smile at him ever so slightly, presents itself.

Great - first pointer won, we got his attention, for sure.

Assuming you were able to smell a cologne - his cologne - did you like what you smelled or did it repel you ? Was it a "loud" overpowering scent, possibly harsh, not to say aggressively attacking your nostril, causing you to take a step back ?

Or was it a fragrance that smelled so delicious, you took a deep breath, inhaling it through your nose and couldn't get enough of it, wanting to get even closer to him ?

Whatever you smelled, should you've been able to notice a cologne, he chose that fragrance because he likes how it smells. Cologne allows the first glimpse into his taste; and what he is about.

Men using way too much cologne one can smell throughout the entire cafe', are either men who like to get a lot of attention, which they get wearing too much cologne.

Or they don't like how they smell, maybe afraid they stink, thus try to cover up what they perceive as their own stink, with lots of cologne. Perhaps a chain-smoker aware his clothes smell of cigarettes. Or, they don't shower regularly, thus instead of soap and water they perfume themselves to try and smell clean.

At first smell, regardless if it's a lot or just a whiff, important is you like it.

Perfumes and colognes smell different on every skin. A perfume/ cologne can smell on one person like an insect repellent, while on another person it smells delightful. That's due to the body's chemistry. But there are colognes and perfumes so harsh, so loud, definitely emitting a toxic smell so bad, it literally attacks your nostrils and causes your eyes to burn and tear.

It has nothing to do with allergies; non-allergic people with all their senses in tact will react to these colognes and fragrances, because of a toxic ingredient. Thus it's not an allergic reaction, rather a natural reaction to a toxin. And these toxins can cause your nose to run, your eyes to water, give you a throbbing headache and cause an adverse reaction with symptoms of mood-changes, and ..... aggression.

If a body is repelled by a toxic smell, the body fights against it when not getting away from that smell - the body/mind reacts; a person suddenly starts acting aggressively. Smells have an enormous effect on our demeanor. They can calm and relax us, entice and allure us, or make us angry and aggressive.

A lot of people take antihistamines for common allergies; antihistamines prevent natural immune reactions, thus those taking antihistamines won't experience any symptoms to toxins, such as burning, runny nose or watery eyes. But they may well experience mood changes, or aggression due to the body rioting against the toxin.

Folks taking a lot of vitamin supplements, in which are quite often antihistamines as well, because some of these supplements are not always what they're made out to be - thus to assure the body doesn't react negatively, antihistamines are added - ergo, they won't experience common symptoms to toxins, either, when wearing toxic fumes; still, their moods change.

How often women, as well as men, wear perfumes/colognes and use soaps, shampoos actually causing them their allergies, is startling. And the moment they stop using the shampoo, or whatever may've emitted the irritant, the allergies go away.

Ever know couples who really like each other, but they can't stand being with one another ?

Though there are certain types of men ( women, too) who're naturally aggressive, or have a temper; some who've never shown a temper or aggressive demeanor with either men or women, ( nor taking medications ) but start acting strangely around the new girlfriend who always wears that insect-repellent Perfume, then it's the perfume setting him of.

Men, in general, are much more sensitive to smells than women, for the most part. This is due to women's wearing of make-up and nail polish; nail polish is very strong and sniffers use it to get high. But women wearing nail polish are so used to that smell, they no longer perceive it as strong after a while.

Make-up, especially powders and lip-gloss with synthetic fragrances are directly applied to the skin. These synthetic floral scents or fruit flavors are on the skin and lips and right under the nose. We may not consciously smell it after a while, but our noses continue perceiving the scents, which, in time, dull our smell-sense, disabling us from perceiving light-fragrances. Ergo, strong perfumes or strong smelling soaps, shampoos, conditioners are bought and used, because one can't smell the lighter-scented items. And these heavy duty fragrances can repel sensitive men.

When a sensible man perceives a perfume of a woman it will either repel him or attract him. If it's a loud/harsh perfume he won't even come near her for several reasons, not just because of the toxic reactions.

Perfumes reflect the personality of the woman. If it's but a hush of a 'clean' scent, then she's a sensible woman; sensitive to herself as well as to others. If it's a flowery scent then she's trying to appear sexy; appealing to men by projecting sex-appeal. Flowery = flirtatious - attract to pollinate.

Women wearing strong perfumes, causing ones eyes to tear, well, they cause your eyes to tear; they'll end up making you sob. When getting a whiff of a harsh, loud, aggressive perfume, then a sensible man will perceive her to be a harsh, loud and aggressive woman.

That perfume could very well be delicious if used in small quantities - a drop behind each earlobe and a drop on the erotic cleft, between the clavicle bones - but when spraying it all over the body from head to toe, after the shower, and another load sprayed over the clothing, one can't but wonder why she seems displeased with her own natural scent ?

If you wish to attract a sensible man with whom you can have a harmonious and sensual relationship - someone who'll like you for who you <u>really</u> are - what's wrong with just a nice clean shower and maybe a hush of real vanilla extract ( not Vanilla perfume ) behind your earlobe ? He'll be wondering what it is about you that makes you smell so delicious, he can't resist wanting to hug and kiss you.

The natural smell of our skin is caused by what we eat. Remember Garlic man ? Yep, oozes right through the pores, doesn't it ? Not the fragrance to wear when on a look-out for his Queen of hearts. Same goes for us females; if you ate garlic, best to chew some parsley afterward; it will neutralize the smell.

Instead of strong smelling body lotion, why not use some coconut oil in moderation ? It's very nourishing for the skin, making it soft and an alluring scent to quite a lot of men. Or any natural oil - if clogging the pores, why not clog them with something your body can digest and is kissable at the same time, with him licking his lips afterward ?

You wouldn't take a sip of that body lotion, even if it smells of bubble gum, so why rub it into your pores ?

You may want to try out different natural extracts, like vanilla, almond, cacao, passion fruit, etc. using <u>just a drop</u> behind the earlobe and a drop on the erotic cleft. It can never repel anyone because there aren't any other ingredients in there a good nose will perceive, especially no toxic smells.

These extracts cost a few dollars, affordable to most everyone and available in every supermarket, as opposed to some perfumes with price tags of $100.00 plus.

Aside from that, nowadays it's a tough guess if you even got the real perfume of a famous label, or a knock-off for the same price, with counterfeits sold everywhere, on the internet and sometimes finding themselves on the shelfs of haute-perfume stores, too.

I do understand that it's chic to some, wearing expensive perfumes of labels. But smells have the tendency to either attract or repel;  it's entirely up to you if you want to smell 'expensive', or Delicious.

# When Weather shapes the Mood

We're at the coffee place and didn't smell a cologne from the possible Mr. Right Guy, but he smiled and we smiled at him, when we picked up the sugar that had accidentally fallen to the ground, right in front of him. Now all we gotta do is go back to our table and wait for him to get up the courage to come to the table, on which we're hopefully not sitting with a male friend, nor a bunch of girlfriends.

Thus assuming we're alone, we sit down and if we tickled his muse he'll come to the table and introduce himself, or sit himself next to our table to assure himself a look from us, encouraging verbal contact.

And, sure enough, Mr. Possible Right Guy sits himself at a table across and woopa our eyes meet again. If he now asks :" Do you come here often ? " , then you know right away you're dealing with a dull guy who smiles at every girl and chats it up quickly hoping for a hook-up, as it's vogue nowadays. It's someone who's lonely, doesn't really know what kind of woman he likes and any girl is just another girl to him with which to spend his lonely hours.

If he comments on the ' weather ', however dull that may sound, it's actually an invitation to get to know you, because preferences about the weather allow the first glimpses into one's personality.

Let's say it's a gorgeous summer day - the sky is cloudless and blue, the sun is shining and the temperature is not too hot, just perfect. If he conveys what a gorgeous day it is, and mentions how he loves the sun, then he most probably has a "sunny " personality, 'cuz he doesn't shy the sun.

This allows for a question, thus gal asks:" How do you feel about cloudy days ?"

If he says something to the extend, " They're ok, too, but i prefer the sun", then you're dealing with someone who takes the things as they come, but knows what he wants.

If he'll say something like, " I can't stand it when it's cloudy", then we may be dealing with someone who has mood changes and is not his own self when it's cloudy. Cloudy days can be used allegorically 'cuz there aren't just sunny days, when all is mighty dandy, in a relationship. Sometimes there are upsets in life - a loss of a job - an illness - or disagreements, and such days are the cloudy days of life and in relationships.

If he can't stand cloudy days, period, how is he going to deal with some upsets ? Will he remain calm in a disagreement, sit down and discuss it, or will he run out the door and you're left with solving the problem 'cuz he doesn't want to deal with it ?

Will you end up tip-toeing around him when there's some stress in the office, which he's unwilling to discuss ?
Ask a follow-up question, as in , " How about winter or autumn ? You enjoy the four seasons ?

" Nah", he says, " I can't wait for winter to be over and autumn is ok when it's sunny, but other than that i really just like it when it's sunny.

It so happens that this conversation is taking place in New York City where one experiences extreme weather changes, thus it's only natural to ask if he lives in the city. If he says yes, you might want to ask why he didn't move to Florida, California, New Mexico, or Hawaii if he's not a season guy ?
And how does he deal with the winter ?

He then let's you know that he's divorced, his ex and kids live in the city, thus he can't live too far away, and though he thought about moving, his job is here, too and he gets really depressed during the winter. I suggest, start working on your comedy act to cheer him up during the winter, otherwise you'll end up frustrated, possibly depressed by his constant complains about the winter, and how cold it is outside.

" Yo, Mister Cave man, the weather is outside and we're inside with the heater on, making it warm and cozy, with a roof on top the building preventing the snow to fall into our living room. And will you look at that lamp bringing light into our cave ? "

Some people just don't know how lucky they are and use the weather as excuse for their discontentment. Of course sunshine is a wonderful thing, it uplifts our spirit; but in a world with roofs over our heads, heaters in our apartments, umbrellas to prevent our hair from getting wet, oil-jackets and rubber boots, how miserable can one be to not recognize how fortunate we are ?

These folks should be sent to the Tennessee hills for a month, where people still use outhouses and may not even have running water inside their homes, having to pump water into their buckets at the well outside, to fill their wooden bath tub.

Not to mention the various transportations available to us, from Bus, to Subway, Taxi, Car , with heat and air-conditioner, not even having to walk through cold, heat, wet, rain or snow.

Assuming you're sitting in California, it's a gorgeous summer day and he complains about the weather: " It's hot today, i'm glad when the summer is over, i can't stand it."

It turns out Mister Gloomy prefers cloudy days and lives in southern California. Why ?

Don't know about you,  but for me the conversation would be over.  I will  look at my cell-phone, ... oops it's already for 3 o'clock, i gotta get going, was nice chatting with you, good bye.
Desperate girl, however, may continue talking with Mr.Personality and Mr. Gloomy and since they're just as lonely as she is, they may even start dating and are happy to have someone they can be miserable with because .... misery loves company.

I don't mind being alone.......
only Misery loves company

# Clairvoyance at the Diner

Gladly, though, this was just a hypothetical scenario and Mr. Possible Right Guy, said, cloudy is ok, but he prefers sunshine.

Of course you could right away drop all the diplomacy and bluntly ask him if he's single. But why not get a few more glimpses into his personality. :
" You're wife likes the sun, too, i'm sure ?"

He tells you he's not married and you spontaneously quip:
" Oh, i'm sorry to hear that. "

That allows for a variety of responses from him and each response will tell you a whole lot about the fellow.

" Sorry ? Why sorry ? ", he asks

To which you'll say: " Because you have no one to come home to and irregular sex is really bad for the prostate."

Hopefully he has a good sense of humor and grins - it should immediately break the ice and he'll volunteer if he's divorced, why he's not married, if he has a girlfriend or if he's single.

If he's a young man up to 52, and he's single and has never been married, it's fine. Men who really know what they want may wait until the right woman comes along, which also shows they don't compromise and that's a nice character trait.

If he's over 52 and single and has never been married, there are few answers that allow for an OKAY status - Artist, Writer, Army, oversees worker, Sailor, Playboy, King of Lalapaloosa who needs to find a royal.

But in the majority, outside of guys who made the decision not to have a family/kids, it evokes curiosity when never having been married while older than 52.

There may be some commitment issues, personality issues, perhaps a bit too kinky for the territory, mother issues, or the Thailand traveler with a preference for transgenders, or, or, or - it's a list of endless possibilities.

If he still seems interesting and not peculiar, there may be another reason, which will reveal itself in time, thus let's allow a chance to learn more on a casual date for dinner.

Mister between the age of 53 and 59, is single, has never been married but seems really charming, has nice teeth, is well groomed, a nice voice ( why else would you continue talking to him ) and the two of you make a date for dinner. A casual little restaurant is picked, where you'll meet him.

Best for a first date is a good Diner because the menu has a greater variety of dishes than specific restaurants like Italian, Chinese, Thai, etc. The first date, in my humble opinion, doesn't have to be a glamor spot where either feels forced to dress to the ninth. For a very first date, lunch or dinner, a casual setting that allows for casual dress and conversation, is far more effective to get a glimpse into the other's personality.

If he's wearing strong cologne meeting you for dinner, then he lacks the senses allowing him to indulge in food, and is more concerned about how he smells, than what the food smells and tastes like. That gives you already plenty of hints about his senses = sensuality.

Thus here you are, at a Diner, and you both take a look at the menu. There's a lot on the menu, lots of different dishes, to choose from; italian dishes, exotic dishes like mango, curry or peanut chicken, or all American dishes like hamburger and steak - fish, salads, omelets ( only at Diners), or soups.

Does he know what he's hungry for ? Does he always look for a specific dish, because no matter what restaurant, he'll pick chicken for dinner ? Or is he allured by what he sees on the menu ? How long will it take for him to choose a dish ? Can he make up his mind, easily, or go back and forth between fish and soup ?

Whatever dish he chooses, the first most important glimpse into his personality is how he talks to the waiter or waitress - how he treats people.

Too nice to a waitress, especially young waitresses, amounts to insecurity on his part where he seeks her recognition of being charming, or tries to get your reaction, while totally inconsiderate for his own ego. That sort of attitude is immature game playing and if a man hasn't dropped such conduct after age 15, he should be dropped.

If he treats a waiter disrespectfully, as though the waiter is his inferior, then he's probably someone who's never achieved the success in life he dreamed of having and tries to project superiority on everyone around him.

Someone like that will treat his mate, his girlfriend, future wife at some point, disrespectfully, too, acting superior or trying to make her insecure about herself so he can feel superior.

People treating others disrespectfully have in actuality no respect for themselves, and to cover that up try to ' project ' superiority. It's a tell all attitude, really.

The one we took to the Diner, however, treats the waitress or waiter respectfully, knows what he wants and chooses a dish, you, too could enjoy - but not today, 'cuz today you're hungry for something else.

*Note

A certain commonality in taste is important. Because taste is not exclusive to just food; it's about everything in life. Every single preference of our senses provides a glimpse into our personality. Example: someone who enjoys spicy foods = hot - delights in hot colors like red or orange. Their sexual appetite is thus more in the hot region, as well.

Best to chew a mint-leave after brushing your teeth before going to bed at night, when waking up next to Mister Tabasco Man, so you'll have delightful morning breath, * wink, wink.

If you're not too keen about sex, then the man of your dream's favorite color is a pale blue, his favorite dish boiled chicken breast with gravy, a side of carrot and pees, from the frozen dinner section of the supermarket, to be heated up in the micro-wave.

But back to the Diner. Some of you reading this may say to yourselves, " A Diner ?" What in the world ? I should be worth more to a man than taking me to a Diner !!! For a first date he should take me to a nice restaurant !!! "

Of course a nice restaurant is a lovely place for a " romantic " dinner. But we're not talking about someone you've known from the office for a long time, with secret crushes having been revealed and him finally asking you out on a date.

You know who Mr. Office guy is, his first and last name, where he works, his office personality, etc. We're talking about a fellow you just met in a coffee place and all you know, thus far, is his first name, maybe even his last name, that he's single and has never been married at the age of 56.

To keep a casual distance while getting to know a little more about him, and he about you, a Diner is the perfect setting. It's a relaxed place where you can leisurely converse while eating, plus no martinis served, nor a bottle of wine during dinner. Staying sober until some mutual trust is assured is the first thing parents should teach their daughters when they turn into teenagers.

Once the dinner is served it's important to watch what he does first.....
Without first tasting the food, he grabs the salt shaker and puts salt over the entire dish. He hasn't even tried if the mashed potatoes need any salt and puts salt over everything.

A person who immediately, without first taking a bite, salts his food, will have a tendency to high blood pressure 'cuz of too much salt. He'll have soft wrinkle-free skin, due to more water content under his skin, but his temperament will be tough to deal with.

He's the kinda guy who starts yelling violently, throwing a temper tantrum in the car, when a car in front of him doesn't start driving fast enough once the light turns green. He's the kinda guy you can have a yelling match with at your hearts content.
Aside from that, " putting salt on everything " can also be interpreted allegorically, meaning he knows how to turn everything ' negative ' - he'll have something nasty to say about everyone = he makes things ' salty'.

Whereas a fellow immediately grabbing the tabasco bottle (hot sauce) likes to 'spice' things up a bit.

Let's assume he ordered something that sickens you to even look at - something you feel repulsed by, unfathomable how anyone can even eat something like that, like pig ears, for example ( in case you're a very visual person ). It's highly unlikely you could kiss someone with delight when repulsed by what he eats.

It would take far more than trying to look beyond it, because it's impossible to look beyond it when lips touch, with you knowing some pig ears where earlier chewed and mushed inside the mouth you're about to kiss; because for very visual people it's a visual that stays in the mind and won't go away. Try erasing a picture from your mind; it's virtually impossible.

A friend of mine, who happens to be a very visual fellow, met a girl with whom he was really taken. Gorgeous girl, great figure, delightful personality; they went on a date and boy was he smitten.

Some time later she invited him to her home where he met her dog and after that it was over, because she allowed the dog to kiss her on the mouth - lick her lips, and my friend had such an adverse reaction witnessing that, he was nauseated, and rightfully so. Who'd wanna share one's lover's lips with a dog ?

Yes, a dog lover, not having problems to kiss her dog may be upset insisting a dogs mouth is cleaner than the mouth of a human being. Who in the world told you that, and why would you even believe it ?

Ever witness a human being licking him/herself clean after going to the bathroom ?

If you're a Vegan and your Diner date first munched on his appetizer of spicy chicken wings, followed by a medium rare hamburger, which totally grosses you out, being a vegan; best to first inquire if someone is a meat eater before going on a date.

Assuming you're not a vegan, nor vegetarian, and this possible Mr. Right Guy ordered a steak, mashed potatoes and a salad and did neither add more salt, prior to tasting it, instead just a pinch of salt and pepper AFTER he took a bite of the steak. Terrific. Now we shall watch how he ' chews ' his food.

Aaah, he closes his mouth, chews it thoroughly and moans a bit, after which he comments on how delicious it is, offering you a taste of the steak. I kid you not, but by the way someone indulges in food, it provides an insight as to how he makes ..... love.
Just listen closely to the sound when he chews, allowing the flavors to dissolve on his tongue and imagine you're being intimate with him. A fellow exuding slight moans, delighting in food, is a " sensual " guy.

If he's someone chewing with his mouth open, even talking to you while he's chewing, then he has zero self-awareness, no manners and is thus unable to be considerate.

A person who's unaware how unappetizing it is for others is to see the chewed up food inside the mouth can't be considerate because you can only be thoughtful when knowing what's commonly offensive.....
to most people. Not every person is repulsed by watching someone talk with his mouth full, specifically folks who do it themselves.

Someone who chews with open mouth, didn't throw his paper cup into the garbage and left it on the table, back in the coffee place, for others to clean up after him.

But if he happens to be chewing with open mouth, don't let it annoy you and entertain yourself. Don't look at him while he's chewing and talking at the same time and stare at your plate while listening. When he takes a break from talking, suggest for him to add some carrots to create a more colorful composition, maybe some of the greens, too and oh, hand him a leaf from your salad, or a piece of parsley and :

" Some garnish to hang out of the side of your mouth, to give it some panache ?"

The most important thing in life is to never create regrets; thus even unpleasant situations should be taken as a great challenge for you to get some entertainment out of it, and walk away from it with a smile, knowing you had yourself some fun.

It's a far more pleasant experience than feeling angry, getting up from the table after you told him how disgusting it is to look at him while he's talking with his mouth full. Worst even when having to listen to the noise that sounds as if sucking on three candies at the same time.

Elbows don't belong on the table, either, while eating. When a man has his left elbow on the table while forking the food with his right hand, he's a rogue. If you're into rogues, who don't have a problem lifting up the skirt, or pull down the pants, of the female gas station attendee in the alley-way, to take her from behind for a quickie during lunch break, then Mr. Elbow man is your kinda guy.

Surely you're wondering by now, how and why i would know all these things and that i must have conquered quite an unaccountable number of men. Actually i just pay naturally a lot of attention to little details - it's genetic - and always link it to intimacy and sexuality.

As a woman watching a man's behavior i grin to myself and often chuckle when observing certain features, behaviors and how it may projects itself during intimacy. It's very entertaining to me, as you can imagine.

I frequently fly and whenever i'm on a plane i can't wait for the landing. It's the highlight of any flight to me, and pay absolute attention to how the pilot lands the plane, relating it to love making, which either cracks me up, or entices me.

When the plane comes down too fast and one feels how it touches the ground real hard, bouncing over the runway - then golly gee, he's a 3 second lift off.

When the plane comes down way too fast, bounces over the ground and has to get back up in the air for a second try-landing - then he's a pull-out, but .... oops too late, he couldn't contain himself.

When the plane comes down too slow and almost crash lands - then i can imagine it was already over before it even started.

When leaving the plane, the Pilots usually stand at the exit to say good bye to the passengers, which i'm always looking forward to, to see what the landers look like. You can imagine my grinning at them, after having experienced the landing ?

And then there are pilots, Holy Shmoly with a Canoli, ....... the plane comes down at a PERFECT speed and you don't even feel it already touched the ground - he lands the plane so smoothly, it's truly an arousing experience and i sigh, look at my seat neighbor and say with my cheeks still blushing and a hush between my words, "Aah, was THAT a great landing", and would light a small cigar, if smoking was still permitted.

These master Pilots of landing are always the mature ones with a certain je ne c'est quois to which all women positively respond ; gray hair - wisdom corners - a strong chin, masculine voice with a *timbre ( *a purr below the breath) and a twinkle in the eyes. So much for the little example with which one can have fun, even on flights, relating it to ye know what.

But now back to the Diner.

Both of you are conversing during dinner and so far all is well and your Diner date is still on the list of being a possible Mr. Right Guy. So far he hasn't shown any oddities that made you cringe and though you're aware he's, say, 56 years old, single and has never been married, there's no indication that he's a madcap. Therefore, it's important to closely listen what he talks about and wishes to voluntarily divulge about himself.

If he starts talking about how successful he once was, driving big cars, having had a big house, a multi-million dollar business, but lost it all because someone cheated him - his stockbroker ran away with his money - the market went bad - a girlfriend took advantage of him, etc. = the usual blame game of others having ruined him, with no fault of his own - then it's needless to say that he's trying to impress you, while fully aware he currently has nothing with which <u>he believes </u>he could impress you.

( I'm sure i don't have to mention that a man just nipping food of your plate,  especially without asking, is a user. )

Any person, be it man or woman, talking about their material status and successes or former successes, believing it to impress someone, is a shallow person who's him/herself impressed by a material status. Anyone talking about " successes " on a first date , is someone regarding you with respect only if you're " materially " accomplished.

I don't say this lightly, but only those who neither have a passion for something, nor a "dream" for themselves, talk like that.

Same goes for men talking about their supposed current success on a first date, the HUGE business deal they're about to strike with a well known company, a well known Mogul, while name-dropping some well known persons with whom they're in business or very best friends.

Whoever is impressed with folks talking a lot about their business successes, who they know, are birds of the same feather.

Common sense will tell ye that a truly successful person, who may be friends with well known people, won't feel the need of having to talk about it. The more successful a person is, in having achieved their dream, the more modest they become. As the old expression goes, ' You don't flash what you have' .
But even with those kinda guys ye just gotta have yourself some fun, because as boring as it is to listen to a bragger, it's a great opportunity to entertain your muse.

Start bragging and make stuff up to humor yourself : " I feel you - i know exactly what you're saying. Good Goat, twenty years ago i won 35 million dollars in the lottery and what did i do ? I spent it like there's no tomorrow, bought myself a Lamborgini ( in New York City) and forgot i don't have a garage. So,... i bought myself a Penthouse on 5th Avenue overlooking Central Park, met a guy who told me he is a money manager and could increase my wealth, and ...gone.

All the money and the guy is not to be found. Now i'm back living in my walk up in Chelsea.

I TRUSTED that man ( pretend to sob a bit, get the napkin to wipe your phony tears ) - he promised we'll live in St. Tropes or whatever that city in Monaco is called ( LOL ) and he ran with my zillions."

Now, quick mood change - look straight at him and : " Just kidding " * mischievous grin.

One of the most unattractive traits, to me personally, is when meeting someone and i'm immediately asked : " What do you do for living ?" - before inquiring my first name. It really puzzles me what it is that behooves a person to inquire about someone's job first and for what reason ?

It's not curiosity about one's " profession" - a craft, art or science one masters. Nor what one majored in in college. But that, too, should politely be inquired about after introducing oneself and asking one's first name.

The ones asking the ignorant question, " What do you do for **living ?"** receive the educational answer from me = "Breathing, eating, drinking fluids".


The Dumbest thing one can say is , " I am smart "

The more we pay attention to what someone talks about, the more we see what the person is really about because we all speak into a mirror; what we see and say about the world and others says more about ourselves than about the world and other people.

Assuming that instead of being a shallow bragger, our Diner Date, talks about how he sees the world, which, according to him, has become this horrible place of but corruption and thievery.

If that's how he perceives the world as a whole, not even leaving a tiny space for some of the beauty and goodness that exists, then he just revealed that he has either been, or still is, ' corrupt ', may've engaged in theft or con-artistry, a Gigolo, thus reflecting the knowledge of himself on the entire world.

We're only able to see the world through our very own eyes. If there's no goodness inside us, we can't see it around us, either.

A thief thinks everyone steals and will be the first to place bars on his window and locks on his doors, fearing someone will steal from him. A cheat will always assume everyone else is cheating, too, especially his mate.

The reason why cheaters are the jealous types, constantly suspecting and accusing the partner of cheating. He can't see the innocence in hugging a friend, amicably talking to a stranger, waving hello to the young neighbor - young enough to be our son.

But in this age of Cougarisms, formerly known as Mrs. Robinson syndrome, a cheater will suspect cheaters everywhere because cheaters can only project themselves.

While conversing with your Diner date, take a look around the Diner and pick a spot in the restaurant where you'll rest your eyes for a few seconds longer. Not the ceiling, though; something on eye-level like the window, the counter, an ornament, decoration.

If he's the jealous type he'll immediately turn his head to where your eyes are resting, to see what you're looking at. If the restaurant is crowded, chances are there's a man sitting in the direction in which you're looking. The jealous type won't even notice the ornament you're actually paying attention to, rather a man in the room, he believes got your attention.

He'll ask you :" Do you know the guy ? "

Which befuddles you because you haven't even noticed any man, thus you inquire in return :" What guy ?"

If your Diner date is an outrageously jealous person he'll be upset and insist :" Like Hell you don't know what guy i'm talking about ! The guy you've been starring at for the last 10 minutes " ( even though it was not more than 30 seconds, but exaggeration is natural to jealous people ).

In this case his name may be Mr. Dippy, thus you'll let him know what exactly you looked at :" Mr. Dippy, dear, you see that delightful flower-arrangement over there ? That's what i was looking at, wondering if it was real or plastic."

Mister Dippy is now embarrassed and so he should be. Jealousy doesn't make for happy relationships.

When a man starts bragging how he's saving the world, sharing that he wants to go to Sudan, Haiti, start non-for-profit orgs., and only sees poverty, suffering and wars, then he's most likely going through some hard times and lost control of his own world.

Everyone encounters some challenges occasionally, or tough times; one starts sorting out the problems and continues doing the best one can to straighten it all out. When procrastinating to solve problems, the problems increase until it gets out of control  - it becomes overwhelming. Instead of at least trying to take control of one's life, some folks run away from it and want to save..... The World, instead - the Whole World, while in actuality they just want to save their own personal world.  Their personal world is falling apart, thus THE World is falling apart for them. All they see is havoc, suffering, etc.

Tom Orrow is a friend of mine.......
problem is he's a Procrastinator

I'm not talking about the young Physician working for Doctor's without borders, nor third world workers, or someone who is doing very well for himself and organizes a food-line for homeless people, because he wants to give back.

I'm referring exclusively to the Mega-goody two shoe who only talks about saving the world in which he sees nothing but suffering to the extreme. There's a girl out there for him, too, who's going through the same turmoil; but they'll never stop to smell the roses, 'cuz even on the roses they'll only see lice.

Ever witness people littering ? Throwing a candy wrapper onto the side walk, drop an empty soda bottle on a hiking trail in the forest, or throw an empty plastic bottle out of the car parked next to a sidewalk, etc ? These folks will end up obsessing when they see dog-poop on a walk way and a cigarette butt in their parking space.

Their lives will be preoccupied with noticing every speck of dirt around their property, their office and start complaining about the dirt hole that's our planet on which we all live. They'll call the city's sanitation department every few minutes when they're older to complain and in their senior years they'll volunteer on weekends picking plastic bags and such, out of the ocean.

The beautiful irony of life.

When pointing the Index Finger at someone.......
three Fingers point at oneself

Sweet Tooth anyone ?

Our possible Mr. Right Guy, however, is none of the sort. He listens attentively when you speak and isn't sharing anything about his occupation, instead he asks you about your hobbies, what you enjoy doing in your free time. You discover common interests of music genres, sports perhaps, and he even has a great sense of humor, i call the 8th sense.

After all, humor must be a sense, why else call it a sense of humor ?

Let's move to dessert. Care for dessert ? Does he have a sweet tooth ? If so, let's see what he orders. If you're a warm apple tart kinda gal, you're a homey person who likes to stay home on the weekends and wish you could be with a fellow to cuddle up under a blanket, both of you contently reading a book.

You wouldn't mind watching a ball game with your mate, while snuggling next to each other on the couch, nipping and dipping finger foods. If he picks an apple tart, he's your kinda guy.

If he asks you if you want to share a desert, because he's pretty sated from dinner, it shows that he's not a glutton nor wasteful. He'd like a bite or two of something sweet, but knows he won't finish the entire dessert, thus to assure it's not going to waste, he asks if you care to share a dessert.

Can you two decide on a dessert you both like, or will one party have to compromise ?

A lemon meringue pie may well be a refreshing dessert of a sweet sour combo; ye might want to ask if that's his favorite ? If yes and he tells you that he always eats lemon meringue, then he's apparently a sweet/sour guy.

Guys with a preference for sweet/sour desserts, or lime sorbet with whipped creme, can be somewhat neurotic in their younger years, hold on tight to their wallet - which is not a bad thing should you not be good at saving money; he'll do it for you.

They don't spent much on themselves and will drive their first car until they go into retirement ; but they're good family men and very dependable. They need affection and tender loving care and if i continue describing the personality of a lemon-meringue connoisseur, it will soon sound like an ad for a pet-adoption of a standard poodle. Playful, neurotic, dependable, smart and very protective - also very good with kids.

Really exciting, evoking enticement, is when you hear someone order, " Vanilla Pudding", ... right ? Oh yeah, the vanilla pudding guy and all ye can think of when hearing the words Vanilla Pudding, is a man who'll turn a relationship into a sensual hot adventure, .... not ?

If at least he ordered Creme Brûlée - it's vanilla pudding, too, but with a caramelized crust and it sounds far more tempting than vanilla pudding. I could have myself a stand-up comedy act with Vanilla pudding - though vanilla ice scream with hot strawberries cooked with green pepper kernels, is quite an extra ordinarily pleasuring experience for the taste buds.

Then there's Mr. Cinnamon-roll who likes his cinnamon roll with lots of icing. He'll like any danish, dessert roll and cookies as long as they have lots of icing, which basically is a tell all into his private sex life, of which he doesn't have much. Icing is very sweet - craving sweetness and lots of it, means there isn't much sweetness in life; no hugs, no loving, no kissing, no sex.

Those eating lots of sugar do it to award themselves with something they lack in life, and numb their senses.

The more sugar, the number the senses 'cuz sugar causes the pancreas to produce more insulin and insulin numbs the senses (nerves). One may experience a quick sugar high, but that high disappears as quickly as it came, leaving the person tired, numb and unmotivated, thus...... the body craves more sugar. Sugar in the form of sweets, breads or alcohol.

It can have a medical reason, too, of course, for example after having used antibiotics and developing a yeast infection; the yeast wants to grow, thus the body craves sugar. If the yeast is not discovered during a 101 medical examination ( stool test) rashes may develop - yeast rash between the buttocks, arm pits, inner thighs.

If the poor fellow ( or female ) is seeing an ignorant Dermatologist, of which we have nowadays aplenty, and he doesn't realize it's yeast causing the rash - prescribing him cortisone cremes - the rash will get worse, the hair on top of his head starts thinning.

Now he becomes depressed, which is common when experiencing a full-blown yeast infection - plus he's avoiding the sun ( yeast does not like sun ), and is psychologically depressed on top of that, due to the rash, and from having gained weight from over-indulging on sweets, feeling unattractive.

He doesn't dare try to meet a girl 'cuz of the rash. It's a devil's cycle, only because of some ignorant Doctors who didn't suggest some pro- biotics while taking antibiotics, and not diagnosing the rash as a yeast rash.

The sad part in these yeast epidemic cases, from which a great number of men and women suffer - while balding in <u>the center</u> of the top of their heads - is because it's VERY easily treated with anti-fungal medications, like Diflucan or Nystatin.

I just had to add that, 'cuz i knew women and men suffering from the above; once they were treated with the right meds, their hair grew back as well.

That just on a little side note, because many women are afraid to even ask their Gynecologist about yeast infections, thinking it's some form of STD, or feel embarrassed 'cuz they're under the impression it's due to uncleanliness.

No dears, it's from Antibiotics,
or.... sugar/yeast bread/alcohol abuse in some people. Read the ingredients in snacks, etc. thoroughly; when it states <u>Yeast Extract</u>, stay away from it.

With all the desserts available, the milk chocolate Savor will always be on top of the list, 'cuz who doesn't like chocolate ? It's not too sweet, not too tart, not sour at all, melts in your mouth with the flavor staying on your tongue and palate, it's pure indulgence of delight.

I bet ye milk chocolate Savors are great kissers, who'll yumm and moan * snickers.
Apropos ' moan '. It reminds me of a darling joke i heard many years ago; kudos to whoever came up with that joke:

Moishe and Sarah sit at the breakfast table when Sarah suddenly says:" Moish, next time when we're having sex, could you do me the favor and moan a little ?"

Says Moishe:" Now you tell me ? After all these years ? But of course i'll do you the favor ."
Thus a few days later the couple is in the mood again, they have sex, Moishe remembers his wife's wishes and :" OY, vat a day in the office ."

# God invented Humor.......
# to keep tears good Company

I'm sure you agree, humor is the most important part in a good relationship. It will get you through rough times, the stresses of daily life; when times are hard, ye gotta learn to laugh it off.
Laughing is as important as crying; it's very soothing to sob once in a while experiencing sadness, a loss of a friend, etc. and those who have a tough time sobbing, they'll find a way to sweat the salt out of the body to release the pressure.

Be as it may, you and the possible Mister Right Guy finished your dessert and it's time to pay. If he suggests you go Dutch, he already decided that there is not going to be a relationship, or not a serious relationship, or he's just cheap.

Going Dutch is done between friends, colleagues, but when on a casual first date, with a male suggesting to go Dutch, it's usually a clue-in that there's no interest in dating you exclusively ( unless he's just cheap ).

Should you, however, suggest to go Dutch, since after all, it's not a formal date, rather a casual date, it's a sensible thing to do; men and women alike hold jobs nowadays, thus you're just as able to pay for dinner. He won't take it the wrong way, rather sees it as not taking it for granted that man should pay at all times. It's a sensible gesture.

If he's okay with it, don't second guess it, or get into the mode of " Cheap bastard, he should have said no and grab the check".

Hopefully, you've already exchanged emails or tel. numbers by now, 'cuz if you haven't and he voluntarily pays the whole bill, with no questions asked, it may also be a way of him being a gentleman and getting the whole thing over with fast, say good night and think ' good riddance' .

The good riddance part usually occurs when women talk too much. There's nothing worse for a man than having to listen to a woman talk and talk and talk about herself in a self-congratulatory manner of how she's such a go-getter.

It's just as big a turn off as for women having to listen to a male bragging. Women <u>emphasizing</u> their " equality" is instantly perceived as, " No equality at all - she wants to be the boss of the house, can't cook and tell me to take out the garbage."
It's a turn off.

Males who've not been married by the age of 56, as this possible Mr. Right Guy, have observed relationships and marriages of their friends. The screaming matches in some relationships with the Miss wanting to get her way, constantly criticizing her mate who can't seem to do anything right, leaving the male frustrated, with the frustration taking a negative effect on his libido.

When that happens she fears he's no longer attracted to her, while not taking into consideration that she's been screaming too much. Unless he's a Masochist, turned on by a dominatrix wearing spike heels and whipping his butt,  a screaming woman with whom he's experiencing a constant " power struggle", will null his libido.

There's an old saying: When she's soft, he's hard - when she's hard, he's soft.

Truly strong women, capable of taking care of themselves, have no need to constantly remind everyone how ' equal ' they are. ONLY insecure women do that and a secure male knows how to spot them from miles away and stays away from them.

Insecure women, however, are a magnet for insecure males seeking to dominate their mates, to make themselves feel powerful.

If he chooses to pay, ye might want to offer leaving the tip ; it's a fair thing to do on a casual first date. If you wish for a harmonic partnership at some point, ye gotta be a team player. It's a nice gesture in modern times.

On a first casual date we know nothing about the man - nothing about his childhood, his upbringing, what kind of a mother he had. That, btw, is also a great topic to talk about during dinner; inquire about his parents. His relationship to his father, his mother, does he have siblings - sisters ?

Just know that a single child, or youngest child with much older siblings, is most often used to getting A LOT of attention.

Best to say good-night to each other outside the restaurant to leave a little distance between the two of you. Distance makes the heart grow fonder.

Should you've walked to the Diner and he happens to live nearby as well, ye still might want to consider walking home by yourself, just so assure yourself some privacy until some mutual trust develops.

One doesn't have to be mistrustful of every person one meets, anticipating a potential stalker should things not work out. But when allowing him to walk you home, after the first casual date, ye could find yourself in an awkward position to receive a good night peck on the cheek, and when liking him a lot already, you may even ask him up, and..... why ruin something, that could go somewhere, after the first date ?

The reason i mention this is because women often believe that the way to a man's heart is by having sex with him asap; getting him attracted to you by playing the Queen of Kama Sutra. Most guys will ALWAYS try to get into your pants as soon as possible, for several reasons:

1.Because they're horny.

2. Because they're always horny.

3. Because you made him horny.

4. Because they're horny and haven't had sex in a while, seeing an opportunity to finally have sex again.

5. To see how easy you are, and once it's accomplished you may not hear from him again until he's horny again and knows to call the girl he was able to bed day 1 after a casual dinner.

Chances are you'll ruin the " mystery " when taking him upstairs trying to prove to him you're the sex Goddess from Phallus-Ville City, the Capital of Venus. Do yourself the favor and allow him to use his imagination. The reason he smiled at you initially at the coffee place, was because he thought you could be his " dream woman".

Allow him that pleasure to dream about you, <u>imagining</u> the woman you are, the same way he'll allow you the pleasure of imagining him to be your dream man.

Imagination is pivotal to a great and long-lasting relationship because we all have a certain type of person in mind, whom we like, desire and feel attracted to. We project that image on a man the moment we spot him, and a man does exactly the same - project the image of a woman he is attracted to, when spotting you.

As long as he doesn't do something that ruins the image you have of him, he'll be the 'dream guy', while also able to constantly surprise you with actions that are new to you. Same with a man; you'll be his dream girl for as long as you're not doing something that ruins the image he has of you.
If he's a really smart cookie he'll play his own ' get to know you inside and out ' game, which is not really a game, rather a strategy only the smartest most experienced men use when serious about a woman. But more about that later.

A smart man, and gentleman, won't go with you if you invite him to come up to your apartment, after a first casual date. He'll most likely be taken a back. Thus if you really like the fellow with whom you just had a Diner date, best to say gracefully Good- night outside the Diner.

For all we know you already made some plans for the weekend to see each other - go to a movie - see a play - or, etc. thus you both have something to look forward to, moving into the direction of getting to know each other. If he likes you, chances are he'll sent you a text, or email, asking if you got home safely. That's a caring fellow who likes you and had a good time during dinner. He may even add he had a great time, looking forward to see you on Sunday, should you've made a date for that day.

Men are a curious species and with all that testosterone very different than we are; Men are by nature Fishermen, allegorically speaking - they'll go fishing to catch a fish to feel a thrill when spotting a fish - hooking a fish - and then catching it to get it into the boat.

There are big game fishermen and small game fishermen. Big game fishermen fish to get a trophy into their boat, hoping for a huge Marlin, which is equal to a supermodel, with whom they can impress their fellow fishermen.

The Marlin is measured, weight and yoo-hoo, one of the greatest Marlins ever caught, ...that year. They'll take lots of photos with the Marlin to hang them on the wall, and of course post them all over their Facebook page, nowadays.

Small game fishermen fish, in the majority, to catch a fish to then consume it themselves. If the fish is too small they usually unhook it and throw it back into the water.

For each fish there's a different hook - Big trophy fish like Marlin are caught by pulling a glittering fake-plastic fish through the water, trying to get the attention of a Marlin. That fake plastic fish is, in this case, an allegory for a flashy car, a double pair of socks inside the pants, a big glitzy watch so heavy it makes ye wonder how he can lift his arm. Lifting is arm may well be an allegory for...

.......which reminds me; why in the world are there so many Cialis commercials on TV in recent years ? And will you look at the actors cast to play the man in need to pop the elevator pill ?

They're in their mid forties to mid fifties - athletic and healthy looking, bright smile, full head of hair.

Ye never see a mature man in his 60's or 70's, or someone who's balding or bald, in these commercials. Considering that <u>certain</u> types of balding-patterns in males are due to high testosterone, i suppose they don't get cast for Cialis commercials 'cuz they have no need for the rocket lift off enhancer super pill which ....

Narration: " If your erection lasts for more than 4 hours please call a doctor. "

I swear to you, if any man's erection would last for more than a half hour it would be meee calling the doctor for emergency treatment 'cuz of physical exhaustion, instructing him to bring along some gatorade to replenish my electrolytes.

Bringing to mind,... have you ever met a man who told you he can do IT for hours ? Whenever a fellow says something like that, i'm always wondering if he's either trying to find out how long it would take for me to be satisfied, if frigid possibly taking hours - or if he's trying to impress me with his stamina.

That naturally leads me to wonder if he does IT professionally, as in " And ACTION ( camera rolling) Torpedo los."

The best line yet, i've heard from a fellow some years back who tried to pick me up, was :" I could make you cum 10 times ."
Jolly gee ! In one sitting, on a day, in a week, in a month ? Please, do be specific, Sir ?

If only some men knew how they crack a girl up, and i ain't talking Chiropractor. It's sometimes really difficult to keep a straight face, thus i don't and have myself some fun with the one-liners.

If you're not turning into an oil-lamp by just listening to the voice of the man, chances are he isn't going to entice you no matter what he does. All the senses play a part in seducing a woman. The eyes **feel** his look, the ears hear his voice, the nose takes in the whiff coming from his neck, the imagination is inspired by watching his lips, body, hands move in a certain way.

The last thing a woman can possibly be enticed by - unless SO DESPERATE and afraid of being alone - is when he talks about sex and what he can do.

We got to deal with the cards we get.......
best to make sure it's our own marked deck,
to see the hands of those we play with

# His Bearing bares his Soul

Also telling of how sensual a man is, is how he **walks**. Same goes for women. We all have a different way of walking, how we put our foot on the ground.

There's the ' trudge' who first plods his heel to the ground, then flattens the foot to take the next step.
Then there's the 'stomper' putting his foot flat and heavily on the ground, stomping away. Some men can't walk slowly, rather pace away at a speed, what comes to mind are the words Humpty Dumpty.

Not to forget the 'skipper,' who seems to lightly hop from one foot to the other - if in balance and not too skippy it's someone with a jovial personality and youthful way into his winter years.

If he's a ' bouncer' someone who bounces up and down while walking, you're dealing with a prankster who's mischievous if he doesn't bounce too high off the ground. If he's gaining a lot of height while bouncing upward, then he apparently tries to make himself taller, in so many ways, than he actually is. Same goes for Mister Chesty, who appears to be pushing his chest forward, with the body seemingly a step behind.

Remember the Elbow man, also referred to as Mr. Rogue, from earlier ? He walks with his legs so far apart, while the feet are extended outward - left foot at 10 o'clock, right foot at 2 o'clock - it makes ye wonder if he went number 2 into his pants.

While Mr. Timid , whose feet are turned inwardly when walking, seems to try to desperately hold in number 1.

There are a variety of different walks and when paying attention how a man puts his feet on the ground, it allows for a great glimpse into....... exactly.

And mmm, watch the fellow who softly places his feet on the ground, rolling his foot to the tip of his toes, with the other foot already positioned to roll to the tip of his toes, walking so smoothly - not in a rush - not too slow - perfect speed. That's the Pilot who landed the plane so perfectly, ye can only sigh watching him walk.

Is it any wonder i enjoy sitting on a bench in Central Park watching people walk ?

Thus to really get a little bit more insight into a possible Mr. Right Guy, take a walk together. Watch and ' feel ' how he is walking. See if you're both walking at the same speed - if he's too fast, too slow, the same tempo, or if you can naturally and organically adapt to each other's tempo.

There's an ART to dating and a reason why man and woman first have lunch or dinner; it provides a glimpse into the behavior and taste of the other. A reason why taking a walk together is pivotal, too, allowing an insight into compatibility.

Aside from what a man involuntarily reveals about himself during a conversation, his facial expressions allow for glimpses into his personality, as well. Did you just say something funny or humorous ?

How did he react ?
Did he get the joke right away, or did you have to explain it ?
And once you explained it, did he get it ? Is he easily amused or will it take an effort to make him chuckle ?

If he laughs TOO LOUD about a ' humorous ' line, something clever that should actually just cause a grin, accompanied by :" That's funny", then he has either no sense of humor at all and tries to cover that up with roaring laughter ...

...or he didn't really get the wit, but is afraid to ask and embarrassed for not getting it, trying to cover it up with way over the top roaring laughter -

or he's trying to convince you he's a jovial guy who LOVES humor, but his real name is in actuality Mr. Gloom and he lied about the weather, pretending he likes sunshine.

Folks with mood swings have also the tendency to over-react; euphoria can be an indicator, 'cuz a balanced person experiences moments of joy and happiness when something exciting occurs, but is most likely not going to holler about it so loudly, with you finding yourself in the position of trying to hold him back from dancing on the street, or get up in the middle of the restaurant to spread the GREAT news with everyone, ....the great news being the humorous line you just shared.

And right after the high was expressed they come crashing down. The higher a ball is thrown into the air, the greater the weight and velocity when it falls to the ground.

Another indicator to see if it's someone who's dealing with some ' issues', is when a man starts psycho-analyzing and labeling.

Just a few days ago i was picking up some window cleaner in the market, when a middle aged man, not too unattractive, stood himself next to me, after picking up a bottle of ammonia from the shelf.

He suggested ammonia does the job just as good as these window cleaners and it's much cheaper.

I agreed, but shared that i liked the smell and use the window cleaner even on my wooden floors.

We chatted a bit about cleaning and i mentioned that i like it clean, everything stowed away the moment i'm done using something; i like it when it's neat. To which he said that it's obsessive, perhaps OCD when in need to have everything <u>sterile</u>.

What exactly, i wondered, did this fellow hear i said ? I told him i used the word <u>neat ;</u> i didn't say sterile, which is extreme ?

Men who psycho-analyze and label can be harmful; they're usually insecure and uncomfortable with themselves and have, most probably, been psycho-analyzed and labeled themselves, at some point.

Or they've questioned themselves, trying to figure out some issues, reading hordes of Psycho-analysis books and magazines, becoming erudite about psychiatric terms and labels.

If strong and confident enough, and one feels a fellow is worth the time and effort to take on the challenge of <u>freeing</u> him, so he, too, can be comfortable with himself, leading to a stress free and harmonious relationship, great.

But, unless one is really confident about oneself, and<u> mentally strong</u>, an insecure man will try projecting all his issues on the female until she's insecure, believing there's something wrong with her, while he becomes the Dominator playing Gas Light ( the Movie) on her.

Reactions to a joke are telling in so many ways. Everyone has a different sense of humor - that's a given - and each sense of humor reveals an essential trait of a human being's personality.

Some have a goofy sense of humor, others delight in black, macabre humor, some laugh themselves silly when someone slips on a banana peel, others like clever quips, wit, knock, knock who's there, and the list goes on. And then there's the common sense of humor that's funny to most everyone internationally - international humor.

But there's insider-humor, as well. Take ' Seinfeld ' for example, to me one of the funniest sit-coms of the nineties, or of all time ( along with the Sid Caesar show, Cheers and yes Roseanne).

For New Yorkers, big city dwellers of the U.S. living among different ethnicities and folks able to think outside the box, Seinfeld was hilarious, because it was ' inside-humor'.

Surprisingly, though, not everyone thought it funny, especially in the heartland of America. It was a New York show with characters ( Kramer ) one is very familiar with in New York.

And while Seinfeld was not too popular in the heartland, Roseanne was a mega hit in the mid-west and big cities; everyone could identify with the characters and the humor because it was self-depreciating humor of an overweight couple not taking themselves too serious, while getting through life's up and down with a sense of humor.

Point being, great topics to talk and inquire about, " Do you like Sit-coms - what's your favorite Sit-com ?

When discovering the same sense of humor, it provides for the most pleasurable moments in a relationship; enjoying comedic entertainment together, instead of one party constantly appalled by what the other is laughing at.

Possibly even leading to a discussion/ argument just as you're watching an HBO stand-up special of your favorite comedian with your partner interrupting and you're not hearing the punchline.

" Now i didn't hear what he just said . What was the punch line ? "

"Why must you always interrupt when i'm watching ... whatsHisName ?"

Very memorable is when visiting friends at their home, watching a movie, or some TV together, while observing the bickering about their tastes in ..... humor, or entertainment in general.

We've all known couples who are constantly at each other, as in, <u>extreme opposites</u> attract, apparently. Extreme opposites who have zippo in common, outside of one thing, perhaps, otherwise they wouldn't have had any offspring.

Neither has a good thing to say about the other - publicly criticizing the other on every occasion, when meeting up with friends for dinner, or at an event, gathering, etc.

From the moment they meet you think there is no chance in hell they'll last for more than a week.  But they get married...... and have been happily nagging one another for almost 30 years.

Their secret ? They LOVE to bicker. I tenderly call them the Bickersons. Both come from bickering homes and bickering is,....yep, comforting to them, reminding them of home.

When Mr. Bickerson first met Mrs. Bickerson, he was annoyed by every single thing she did, said and how she dressed and fell madly in love.

I imagine foreplay by the Bickersons would be something like so :

She draws the curtains, he says :

" No, let the moon shine in a little and keep the light out. Are you wearing the black thing again ? Why can't you wear the pink negligee tonight ?"

She : " Because i don't feel like wearing the pink negligee."

He: " You're never in the mood for the pink negligee."

She: " So not true, i wore it last week !!! "

He : " And i liked it VERY much, couldn't you tell ?

She: " You, you, you, it's always about you, isn't it  - why don't you put on that cowboy hat, which i like on you  ?"

He: " Because i don't really get a kick out of it when you start calling me Logan or Reid ."

She: " I guess i was being a naughty girl "

He: " Yes you were - a bad bad girl and you need a spanking "

The Key to thrive, enjoy and be.......
is called Consensuality

# What his features say about him

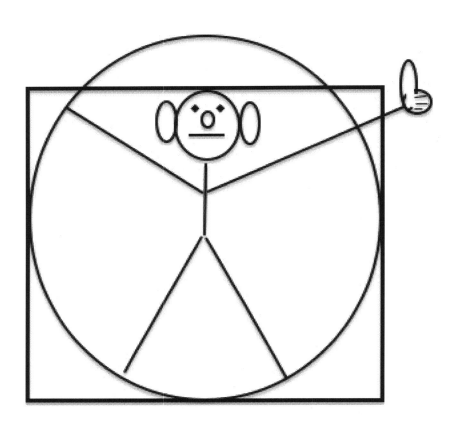

From teeth, to ears, to eyes, eye brows, to chin, nose, forehead lines and hands - each and every feature reflects on the entire person. It's not always genetics creating our bodies - it's the personality we develop causing for our features to eventually change.

Strong eye brows reveal potency, authority, mental strength, and great passion. If you're wondering about the size of the feet, it does not reflect on the size of his Chief Justice.

There are guys with a shoe size 8 and they have a trained python in their pants, very apparent when wearing boxer shorts, and Monty is taking a stretch down his thigh.

Seriously, can ye blame a girl for looking at the fork in the tree, where a man is very obviously drawing attention to by sitting so brought legged like a woman during her annual pep-smear at the OBGYN ?

That's when ye unintentionally notice a Boa Constrictor, and having noticed the serpent, the eyes glance at the shoes, not bigger than a size 8 1/2 and then you know - feet do not indicate the size of his esteemed member.

Not a turn on to me, personally, when a man sits with open legs, well aware he's wearing boxer shorts. These boxer shorts don't hide a thing, unless he's able to sit like a gentlemen, crossing one leg over the other.

Really peculiar, pushing me into wonderment, is when i so happen to spot - in a third of a second glance, of course - a protrusion the size of a grapefruit on his upper thigh.

Now he may well be a ballsy guy, but if his voice sounds like the solo singer of a castrato choir, i tend to second guess that he's indeed in the possession of family jewels of that caliber. Barry White though, i'm sure, hid the jumbo size Faberge Egg collection.

You can get a pretty good look of the shape of ye know what, by closely looking at his <u>thumb</u> and nose.

There are all kinds of thumbs and they're the best indicator of all and everything regarding the shape, width and size, combined with the nose. The Nose is the same length as the Thumb from top to second joint. Each of our body parts corresponds to other body parts.

There are small thick stocky thumbs, corresponding to a short nose bridge. Long slender thumbs correspond to a long, thin nose bridge.Then there are thumbs with a waist and very straight thumbs.

If you like his thumb, chances are you like his…. ye know what.

Bent backwards thumbs - also called hitch-hiker's thumbs, have some meaning, but not if he's an avid guitar or violin player, because a thumb starts bending backwards in time, due to playing these instruments.

Guys with bend thumbs go well with women who have such thumbs. It has nothing to do with sexuality, ( the double jointed thumb) rather a personality trait that maybe a little too far outside of the box for some.

It really comes down to liking what you see. If you see a feature that makes you cringe, something about the man's personality will, at some point, make you cringe, as well, while another woman will be enticed by that feature, resulting in compatibility.

And then there is the thumb ye gotta watch out for ; a thumb with, what's called a <u>toe nail,</u> It's a thumb with a nail bed thats very short and wide.

Such a fingernail can be on one or on both thumbs; it means that such a person has a 'rocket temper' - they can go off in a split second and throw tantrums, it's very difficult to deal with and also relates to their sexual temperament. Sexual opportunism is quite common with men ( and women) who have such thumbs, including utter disregard to others to the point of ruthlessness ; while yet, they can be quite charming if.... it serves their purpose.

Toe-nail fingernails can be on other fingers, too, and each corresponds to a different personality trait. If such a nail is on the middle finger it means the person is promiscuous.

Then there's the thumb-mountain, also called the venus mountain; the elevated part of the thumb inside the palm of the hand. If the elevation is very high and hard, extending from the thumb all the way to the life-line, then it's a very sexual and selfish person. If the same sort of mount is soft and pillowy, he's also very sexual, but not as selfish.

If the mount is apparent on the inside of the thumb, creating a valley toward the life-line, he's balanced, and if that area shows hardly any elevation, then we're maybe dealing with a real monk passionately dedicated to his celibacy.

If his pinky on one or both hands is bend inward, he has masochistic tendencies, likes the Dominatrix style black leather and rubber outfits, and may be watching cat woman movies lashing out with her whip, enticed by the thought of a woman taking charge sexually.

The stronger the inward bend of the pinky, the stronger the tendencies. Curiously enough, corrupt men, making a living lying and conning people all the way to the top, becoming quite successful, often sport the kinky pinky. Ironically they seek to be submissive sexually, and physically being punished by a woman turns them on, thus they go to a Dominatrix. Poetic justice.

Earlobes are one of the features ( aside from noses and nostrils, teeth and oh the list goes on ) i personally pay most attention to.

If you like Rainmakers able to charm you 'till you believe your real name is Melisande, then a fellow with attached earlobes is the right guy for you. An attached earlobe is when the inner earlobe is attached to the facial skin above the jawbone, and doesn't hang loose.

You may be the trophy on his arm he's long been looking for and suited for his need of public acceptance and his own advancing in the public arena, which may suit both of you - but don't expect him to be there for you 100 % when it comes to going through thick and thin 'till God do ye part.

His ego may be a in the way somewhat to be a comforting husband who can nurture your soul in times of need. In public he'll make sure to give that impression, though, since his contentment depends mostly on a positive public perception of him.

Ears can be different on both sides of the head; one ear may be attached, while the other earlobe is loose, thus in the above case, he may well be comforting if he has a non-attached earlobe on his ' right ' ear. An attached left-earlobe would point to a secret part in his personality by which he'll pick a woman for public acceptance, rather than love.

Example: Some men with these earlobes, could, for example, be very attracted to curvy gals, voluptuous women, chubby females.. They may even fall madly in love with them, but they won't marry them because of a public image they wish to project.

Or he's in actuality attracted to a girl who happens to have no higher education, no degrees, but instead marries the girl with an impressive resume', graduate of an ivy league school, to advance his public image. You'll find the majority of people with attached earlobes in the political arena.

But everyone has a different goal in life. If you want to become President of the United States, or the most respected female CEO of a Fortune 500 Company and the whole harmonic relationship thingie is not on top of your list, a man with attached earlobes is well suited for you and you two may have a very <u>successful</u> marriage for life.

We're all different animals and there's a mate out there for everyone. There are just as many A-sexual men out there as there are frigid women who don't care for the intimacy part in a relationship at all; and when these two find one another they have the happiest marriage, going bungee jumping.

There are girls who like to suffer, like that famous song, " Oh so glad to be unhappy". They'll always succeed finding a guy to make them unhappy. They may complain about the relationship and how they're being mistreated, but that's part of what they like.

Bad girls, who've stepped and walked all over men in the past, may want to punish themselves subconsciously and find themselves a guy treating them badly and.... they like it. We've all seen it again and again. Not to forget female masochists.

It always comes down to the Mirror - we give ourselves what we believe we deserve. We choose a man, subconsciously, we feel we deserve at a particular moment in time.

Of course there are legitimate abusive relationships with a woman or man kept somewhat hostage in a relationship via manipulation tactics.

But even in these cases, how often do they go back to the guy, or the girl, sometimes out of opportunism, because the abuser provided for a luxury life style ?

A gold digger who found herself a fellow who happens to be a sadist, but at the same time a ' provider' of a luxurious life style, and thus, regardless how abusive the relationship may seem on the outside, she's willing to stay rather than leave, having to provide for herself.

To some there's the excitement in making up after a fight - again and again. Some women provoke a fight ( as do men at times for the same reason ) only to feel a temporary rejection to then lure him in again, to feed the ego.

Rejection is an enormous aphrodisiac for many women. It's so well known that guys created games, rejecting women, only to lure them in. It works immensely on insecure woman.

Each and every one of these games work on VANITY. And even the most self-confident woman will fall for them IF she's vain.

Fellows playing rejection games with women to lure them in are easily detected by the comments they make, which is usually about something they perceive to be a vulnerability of the woman.

Let's say you have small breast, which many women feel insecure about. You meet a man and on the second or third date he asks you if you've ever thought of getting implants ?

Instead of being taken aback by that question, feeling embarrassed or even share that you've considered it, feel good about yourself and tell him :" For many men a champagne glass full is quite enough ".

If he then states that he prefers women with some chest, tell him that, " There are plenty of women with big boobs out there to chose from - natural, silicone and saline. Why talk to a girl with small breast when in actuality you're attracted to big breast ? "

Some men like big breast, some like HUGE breast, some don't care if it's a DDD cup filled with saline or silicone, others like medium sizes, or small breasts.

There is a man out there who likes you just as you are naturally. The one who is YOUR guy, the perfect match, who likes every single aspect of you.

If you change yourself to suit someone who's actually attracted to a different type of woman, and the relationship falls apart, you'll end up with the triple D's and the one who would be attracted to the natural you, may not even approach you 'cuz all he sees is the triple D's he's not too keen about.

A lot of men can scan false breasts from miles away and don't like em.

Sure you can have the implants removed, but you're left with stretched out skin and tightening, or lifting the breast, will leave scars.

The reason i mention that is because i know young women, who looked really pretty, but fell for guys making them insecure about themselves and they ended having their entire bodies surgically reconstructed.

They became almost unrecognizable, especially in the face, aside from some surgeries gone wrong. It's irreversible, just remember that.

If a man tries to make you feel insecure about yourself and your body, instead of making you feel comfortable, relishing all of what you're made of, then hello ? Unless of course, you want to punish yourself, feeling you deserve to be disrespected. That's a personal choice, subconsciously or otherwise.

There is no perfect body - no perfect human being - no perfect man and no perfect woman. Perfect is in the eyes of the beholder ; perfect to YOU and perfect to HIM may not be perfect to someone else. But there's a fellow out there who's perfect to YOU and you're perfect to him.

It's always befuddling to me why some men ( women, too) are with someone who is not their type and then try changing their mate into a different type they feel more attracted to, even encouraging them to see a plastic surgeon.

The black haired Chinese girl with slanted dark brown eyes, small breasts and a boyish body that's natural to her ethnicity, is turned into a Miss Moldavia contestant.

Her hair is bleached light blonde, slightly breaking the hair-structure because East-Asian hair is the most difficult hair to bleach. She's undergone eye-lid-surgery while wearing Husky-blue contact lenses and her breast turned from a 34 A to 34 D.

And all that because he didn't want to pay for the Moldavian beauty contestant's family's flight because the parents didn't allow their 19 year old daughter to travel by herself to meet Prince Charming from America who could provide for a good life for her and her family.

Instead Ying Chang, who already lived in the U.S. giving violin lessons to his son from a former marriage, was willing to turn into a Slavic looking beauty queen.

While north America is a melting pot of the world with so many ethnicities living together, it's mind boggling why some ethnic men and women feel they have to turn into Scandinavians, unhappy with their features so naturally beautiful to their ethnicity.

It's great to experience a little with hair colors and hairstyles - turning straight hair curly and visa versa - choose a type of look for yourself you feel is more suited for you, to feel comfortable with yourself in the pursuit of your own happiness.

Doing it <u>for yourself</u> and only for yourself, so you and only you are responsible for the changes and take responsibility for it. No one made you change into something or someone you may start feeling discontent with.

When doing it for someone else, however, and the results are either not as you imagined they'd be, or there's a break up, a ' blame game ' ensues.

" Look what you did to me
I changed FOR YOU - I did all of this for YOU
You what ? You're breaking up with me ? After ALL i did  for YOU ? "

We all have our vulnerable spots, which men, playing confidence games, immediately spot and point out to see our reaction. Self-awareness of our bodies helps a great deal to put these fellows in their place. Make jokes about it yourself - that's the way to go.

If i had small or hardly any breast, i'd be bragging how i put any man's chest to shame.

I have big feet, shoe size 12, and the first one mentioning my feet would be me, when i notice someone starring at them. I'd say :" Size 12, and just in case you've heard of big foot, that was me stomping barefooted through the Canadian woods during rainy season, leaving some foot prints.

If the person is now encouraged to let me know that :

" Those are really big feet ",  i'd say:" Like Jesus, he must have had big feet, too, 'cuz shoe salesmen appear to constantly confuse me with Jesus.

He'll then say :" How's that ?"

To which i tell him that every time i go to a shoe store asking for a size 12 pump, the salesman states, " Jesus Christ, you got big feet ."

Point being, humor always breaks the ice and no one can possibly offend you unless you allow them to. It's a choice - you can choose to be offended or be not be offended - it's entirely up to you.

No matter what country or language, when tall there's always someone pointing out you're tall, while uttering the long over-used and old-hat line :" How is the air up there ?

" I keep telling these folks :" It's not about the air. It's about the view
".

Not kidding, i once made myself a t-shirt, some years ago, that read on
the back:
I'm 6 foot 2
I don't play basketball
The air is swell up here, but it's really about the view

A lot of women come up to me and tell me they wish to be 6 feet tall.
They're under the impression tall is the cat's meow because of the tall
model's status. That being tall comes with an enormous amount of
challenges and hurdles is not considered, because they're not aware
of the details.

I always tell them that if a Fairy would grant them their wish, after one
week they'll pray to have their original size back because......

1.With tall comes  bigger feet  for which you'll have to find shoes.
Good luck, 'cuz you can't just go into any shoe store and choose the
shoe of your liking.  Most shoe stores carry shoes up to size 10. To
find a shoe size 11, 12 or 13 you'll have to either pay a LOT of money
in a specialty store for tall people, with the designs not too appealing
to the eye, nor high heels, or a LOT of money for European made
designer shoes, or find outlet stores you have to get to real fast,
because the few left-overs of the season in your size will be gone the
next day.

2. With tall come longer legs for which you'll have to find pants long
enough to fit you. You can't just go into any boutique, clothing or
department store and pick yourself a pair of jeans or dress pants. You
have to find the stores or labels that carry ' extra-long'.

Thus you'll either pay LOADS of money for a pair of pants from a speciality store for tall people, whose designs are not too fashionable, or you pay LOADS of money for tailored pants - or you really have to put in an effort finding the labels and stores carrying your extra-long pants.

3. With tall come longer arms, for which you'll need shirts, sweaters and blouses whose sleeves are long enough. Same as above, good luck.

After one week of trying to shop for clothing - realizing beds aren't all made for tall people either - bumping your head on various things hanging too low - avoiding umbrellas to hit your eyes, you'll experience It's a Wonderful LIfe ( Christmas movie with Jimmy Stewart ) and get the Fairy back its wings once you have your prior height back, thanking the Lord for being so lucky being just the way you are.

As a child, going shopping for shoes with my father, when my feet were already the size of clown shoes, he knew it would be a tough life for a girl with big feet ( my mother was very tall and had big feet, as well ), we'd enter the shoe store and he'd ask the store clerk to direct him to the ' canoe' department to find shoes for his little daughter. He prepared me for the future when i would be harassed, teased and made fun of ( especially in school ) because of my height and big feet, as in …. first know how to deal with hecklers before going on stage.

First know how to extinguish a fire<br>before you ignite a flame.

Back to some earlobes.

There are ears with no earlobes, at all. If both ears lack earlobes you're dealing with someone who takes everything personal - he'll only hear me, me, me - everything is about him - he's the center of the universe and the sun rotates around him, exclusively.

Whatever you may say, " Gosh, i feel fabulous today ", refers to him. He'll say:" You feel great because of me, and don't forget it".

" No", she says ( uh oh don't argue) i feel great 'cuz it's just such a perfect day; my work is all done, the house is clean, i just feel so relaxed ".

To which he'll respond, saying: " So what you're saying is that i have nothing to do with you feeling fabulous ? Why are we even together if i have no effect on you ?"

As you can imagine, this will end in an argument with him seeking confirmation of being the responsible party for her contentment, <u>exclusively</u>. No matter what, everything evolves around him.

Remember, though, both ears can be different and if the right ear has an earlobe while the left ear has no earlobe, then he's a bit more balanced in his egocentricity.

Other than that he may well be a great fellow, though a temper is not unusual for those with attached earlobes, either - still, we're all books with many chapters and egocentricity and a temper is just one chapter that could be a little challenge, if you're unable to deal with it.

If everything else is splendid, have fun with it by starting out with a compliment :
" Because of you, of course, i feel splendid, which is a given my honey pie whose face i adore" - * wink, wink, give him a hug, a kiss - " but having won the Senate seat sure adds to my happiness with you, you, you , sweetheart.

Earlobes that hang very lose, meaning there is absolutely no attachment - not even on the upper part of the inner earlobe - creating a visible long space between earlobe and facial skin, belong to men with extreme view-points, ideologies and insist they're right even when rationality and science opposes every aspect of their believes.

They have a difficult time to trust anyone, thus live isolated lives and ( not rarely ) stay life long bachelors. They seek confrontations where an opportunity presents itself, thus it's needless to say they're not the easiest men to get along with. Having said, if you share his views - congratulations.

But remember, both ears are different and one may have one kind of earlobe on one ear, while the other earlobe is totally different, allowing some balance as far as personality is concerned -  if the good ear is on the <u>right</u> side.

Ears ( and noses ) continue to grow with age and earlobes may grow longer, too. There are different length of earlobes, but they reveal more about the passion for life, one's constitution and longevity than personality traits to look out for.

Men whose earlobes tend to be thick and curl forward have a temperament that can lead to violent aggression. The thicker such a curled forward earlobe is, the more the tendency toward radical views and violence. You'll often see such ears in violent <u>Extremists</u>.

An ear that lays extremely close to the head, belongs to someone who has a difficult time of thinking outside the box, lack of imagination.

Now, one could say that this is prejudice against earlobes and bodily features. I assure you it's not, it's not prejudice, it's post-judice.

But let me rationalize it for you :

If the corners of the lips are constantly downward, due to moodiness or being miserable, the person creates downward lines/ wrinkles extending from the corners of the lips downward to the chin.

If someone smiles and laughs a lot, naturally they'll create themselves laugh-lines next to their eyes and the center of the cheeks. When frowning a lot, you'll create frown lines between your eye brows. If the frown lines are symmetrical it's due to ' concentration ' , whereas unsymmetrical frown lines are due to expressing displeasure, disapproval.

A crooked feature reveals that there's a crooked personality trait, the reason why we use the term ' crooked' for people who're crooked. Villains in movies and comics are always fashioned with crooked features. Even a crooked tooth gives away specific traits of a personality.

Take notice of men with the right front tooth protruding - sticking out - sometimes even somewhat discolored. Did you ever meet such a person and did he talk about himself as caring, sensitive, idealistic, always helping people, etc ?

And did your experience with that person concur with his self-aggrandizement ?

What about someone whose left front tooth is protruding - sticking out ? That's the one who's actually going out of his way to do the right thing; a silent philanthropist, that friend of yours you can always call on, while yet he never brags about his goodness.

Since every part of our body corresponds to another part of the body, as in nose/thumb, or the length of the middle finger/ the length of the forehead, the length of the little finger equalling the length from nostril-divider to chin, the length of the hand = the length of the face, etc.

Each feature allows a glimpse to the parts of the body hidden from view when fully dressed. The circumference of a closed fist equals the length of the foot, etc.

Ever notice a little sharp corner developing on the nostrils of someone getting angry, or argumentative ? These corners are muscular dimples not always apparent, only making themselves visible in either one or both nostrils when the person is displeased or angry.

Caution, you're dealing with an active Volcano. He may erupt soon, or in several years, but he'll erupt; the good thing is a Volcano doesn't erupt silently - first you'll feel a rumbling, some tremors - then you'll see some smoke, and if you've not evacuated the room, or the apartment by the time he's smoking you'll see a Dragon spit fire like you've never thought possible.

That's someone with one corner in the left nostril.

Active Volcanoes can control themselves for a long time - they compromise for the sake of peace and eat their frustration for as long as they can, and won't even as much as confront the issue they're frustrated about ( in the office or at home ) putting their foot down, until one day when it's enough and then, ..... HOLY SMOKE

He may otherwise be a terrific fellow, and if noticing the Volcano is smoking - evacuate the house for a few hours, go for a walk, for a coffee, or to a movie - allow the volcano's eruption to release its pressure, and once that's accomplished it's safe to go home and he'll be his new self, able to finally talk rationally and calmly about what's been bothering him.

If these corners are on both nostrils he can become mean; i mean REALLY mean.

Naturally, certain features combined with other features either enhance a certain personality trait, or make it lesser. Listening to one's gut is always the right decision, no matter what you may feel about features.

And if you're unwilling to listen to your gut-feeling, if the hair on your back stand upright, ... that's the red light signal suggesting STOP.

I've had a fascination with features since i was a little girl. I gave people a cat-scan, as i call it, checking every detail from eyes, eyebrows, ears, nose, nostrils, lips, teeth, fingers, watching their mannerisms, gestures, but also listening to their voices and my instinct.

What originally inspired me to do that were drawings in old fairytale books; the first features that got my attention were the eyebrows of the bad Queen, stepmother of Snow White.

I wondered why her eye-brows were drawn in such a high upward bow ? After some time of paying attention to women with such eye-brows i realized it revealed ' vanity '.  Mirror, mirror on the wall.

Each of the characters in the original Grimm's fairy tale book were given specific features reflecting their personality, and sure enough; when giving folks cat-scans the features did indeed provide a glimpse into their personality. That's what started my fascination with features.

How to find out if feet, thumb/hands or nose reflect on a man's private part ? Easy, ...one travels through Europe and goes into co-ed saunas ( most saunas and steam rooms in central Europe are co-ed) where men RARELY cover themselves with a towel; take some pen and paper along and take notes while visually observing the different features, comparing them to one another.

Even better, wear dark sunglasses so the males don't see what exactly you're so analytically staring at.

Of course i didn't really take a note book into the sauna, but now that i come to think of it, how fun would it be to put up an easel and start drawing, then address a fellow sitting across from you and politely ask:" Sir, would you mind raising one leg so i can get a better look at IT ? "

" Oh and don't worry, i'm not going to draw your face; i do respect your privacy ."

Men, for the most part, are so much more comfortable with their bodies than women, in general. They can have a pot-belly like a women about to give birth to triplets and stick it out with such boldness,  it's refreshing and projects such confidence it instantly makes them attractive.

There's something said for confidence and confident men all have one major feature in common, and that , Monsieur De Bergerac, is a high Nose bridge. The higher the nose-bridge the more cocky they are.

Thus i often wonder what it is that behooves a man to get a nose job to make his nose <u>smaller</u> ? Modesty ?

Which brings me to the word " horny". What feature makes a man look horny - relating to VIRILITY, outside of the Ding-Dong when it's in an uplifting mood, which would be too obvious ?
Imagine a nearsighted person looking at a man with  receding <u>wisdom corners</u>;  it's out of focus, blurry and creates the appearance of two horns; ergo horny.

There are different male balding patterns. Receding ' Wisdom Corners ' does not equal a receding hairline starting at the entire front - nor does it equal when the hair is falling out on top the head, right in the center; the latter is called a Monk's Circle, which also occurs due to advanced Candida ( yeast infection ).

Men, whose hair falls out in the back of the top of their head, however, have a lot of testosterone, too.

If ever you wondered why some women are with men who're balding or bald, and don't even urge them to get hair implants,  a toupee or a wig, now you know - it's testosterone causing <u>male-pattern baldness</u>, as in receding ' Wisdom corners', and a bald spot in the back on top of the head. These balding patterns can appear separate or together, and when together they lead to complete baldness with hair remaining on the side of the head.

They're virile men and due to their virility, regardless of the size of their Chief Justice, very confident males. They're so confident, in fact, they don't even try covering up their receding wisdom corners with left and right over-combs, or bangs. Instead, cocky as they are, they comb their hair back.

And if that fellow can cross his legs sitting on a chair, ( able to comfortably put one leg over the other ), enticing appearance, indeed.

A confident male does not color his grey or white hair. Men coloring their salt and pepper hair fear it makes them look older, thus try to look younger and any man trying to look younger by coloring his silver hair jet black or *dark brown ( *which usually turns orange after the second shampoo ) is either uncomfortable with his age, or wants to attract much younger females.

In actuality the darkened hair, with the white roots showing, make them look much older, because it brings out the lines. while silver or white hair brings light to their face and diminishes the appearance of lines.

The ones coloring their white hair jet black usually end up with women the same age who have ' youth ' issues, as well - thus they're a perfect fit, believing they look young together.

We all want to look and feel young for as long as we can and like what we see in the mirror, feeling good about ourselves; but when over 40, the knee-high stockings underneath the mini skirt, along with pig-tails, are perhaps a bit too young a look that has the opposite effect ?

Same with men going a bit over the top trying to look young:

"That is indeed astounding, Mr. Schmitzelhuber, that you can still fit into the leather knickerbockers you wore when you were 15 years old. And that boyish coif with the bangs, one would never guess you're 78 years old. ".

To lie to others is a forgivable Human trait
To lie to oneself is an unforgivable serious Offense

# The Masculine Voice

When i grew up men had masculine voices. All men i knew - my father, uncles, family friends, teachers, and even the men on TV and in the Movies - had deep voices through which one could distinguish between male and female; when hearing voices on the radio, for example. Females had high voices and males had low voices.

I don't know what it is that has changed, but one rarely hears deep masculine voices, with a timbre underneath the breath, in the United States anymore.

Is there something in our food that causes male voices, specifically in the younger and baby boomer generation, to rise sounding like girl scouts ?

We don't seem to pay much attention to the sound of voices and how it effect our senses, emotions, anymore either.

There are still some men with masculine voices, thank Goat, but they're like gold dust in the desert sand, especially on TV, radio and the movies.

Nowadays, it seems, men and women can have a shrill, high pitched and even <u>nasal voice</u> making one cringe, shudder and get a knot in the stomach when listening to it, and get a job as a news anchor, TV host, or a radio show, which 20 years ago would have been unthinkable.


What ever happened to voice coaching ?

There is a great lack of self-awareness or sense-deficiency going on in our country, ( it does not appear to affect countries oversees from what i gathered through my travels ) and we're apparently not paying attention to how a voice effects our bodies, thus pay no mind to how our own voice sounds, effecting others, and that includes both genders.

The reason i bring this up is because a terrible voice is the second biggest turn off next to bad breath.

The most beautiful woman with a figure like Aphrodite and fragrant like a honey comb will instantly become unattractive to a sensible male who is audio-sensitive, which <u>all the great men</u> out there are. I've witnessed it time and again, with male friends having approached a girl and the moment she started talking the attraction was gone.

Her voice was either too harsh, lacking gentility, softness, ergo <u>femininity</u> - or it was to shrill, squeaking like a machine in need of … **Oil.** Or her voice was high pitched like a jet-engine at high speed, or nasal, that even sweet terms of endearment would sound like whining.

Yes, a man could help her find <u>her</u> voice by suggesting to record herself, then objectively listening to her voice with closed eyes.

The problem is that many women nowadays insist they should be loved for who and how they are, with vanity and ego constantly getting in the way of accepting well meant critiques, to refine her, turning a diamond in the raw into a lustrous radiant gem, like Professor Higgins turning Eliza Doolittle into ' My fair Lady '.

With men it's exactly the same thing.

There he is, Mister receding wisdom corners, wearing a strawberry ice creme colored shirt, the hands inside his pocket, slowly and softly rolling his feet over the ground, suave, debonair, bursting with confidence and masculinity, when suddenly you hear him comment on the magnificent weather, sounding like Woody Allen on Helium.

That's when global warming turned into ice age........

The luscious spring and well instantly drying up, and the only thing preventing a drought of mega proportions is to put in the earplugs of the smart phone, as quickly as possible, find a video on youtube to listen to Lee Marvin singing, ' I was born under a wandering star', before the fertile valley is turned into a barren desert.

It's stupefying why these men, with voices making Peewee Herman sound like a purring Porsche engine, are so perplexed, wondering why they're constantly rejected by women.

Don't they know what they're voices sound like ? So what he looks like Zeus, but when listening to his voice all one can think of is Peter Lorre as Ugarte in Casablanca.

When meeting a man, close your eyes to listen to his voice and allow yourself to _feel_ how it affects you.

If the voice has shriek appeal, record it, play it for him and suggest he should relax his stomach muscles when speaking, releasing the breath while uttering the words, and you'll magically lead him to discover his natural masculine voice, with that oh so enticingly purring timbre.

# The Games

Back to dating: Remember we took that possible Mr. Right Guy to a Diner, had dinner, observed his behavior; the check was paid, you were a good girl and went home after saying good night outside the restaurant.

Now let's assume he sent you a text, inquiring if you arrived home safely after your Diner date. And you replied, telling him all's well, thanks for asking and wished him a good night. Lovely.

Assuming he didn't text or email you, that's alright, too. I wouldn't make too big a deal of it. He has your phone number and email address, but the next day you don't hear from him either. It's odd, 'cuz a well mannered individual would call or sent you a message, saying hi, or mentioning he had a good time.

Fair enough, you sent him a message: " Hi, had a great time last night - how are you ?"

No response - either that same day, nor the next day. Play devil's advocate, 'cuz depending on his profession or schedule, he may've not checked his email yet, and his non-reaction has nothing to do with you. Sometimes it's simple forgetfulness. If he has not replied by day 3, assuming he's well, there may be another reason why he hasn't responded.

The GAME

About ten years ago ' The Game ', a pick-up guide for men, became The Bible for insecure males unable to even initiate a conversation with a female. Of course i bought the book; i was curious what the dogs came up with this time around, trying to trick cats.

Men were advised to basically play the old rejection and confidence games from junior high school and not react to phone calls, emails, nor call a girl after a date. That way, the girls will run after them ( according to the book ) with the guys actually just collecting phone numbers.

Needless to say, these tricks only work on very insecure women and are played by very insecure males. Thus if Mister Diner date has not replied, give him a call, say hello ( maybe he accidentally deleted your email , which can happen, and can't find your phone number, etc. ) and then leave it be.

If you're angry, feel offended or hurt, because he has not replied or contacted you, it's only due to Vanity.

" How dare he ?

Who does he think he is ? "

You're only getting yourself worked up over nothing and if he is indeed playing <u>The Game</u> on you and you may call him, leaving a message to tell him off, it will only feed HIS ego - not yours.

If you have a good conscience, were well mannered and had a nice dinner at the Diner, there should be no reason for you to second guess yourself, nor punish yourself by getting angry. If someone else treats you disrespectfully and it's undeserved, why punish yourself, getting angry and feel hurt ?

Best to see unpleasant things at the very beginning, than when you've become emotionally involved in a relationship. Bad manners are signs - good signs to protect us from real hurt, poetically speaking.

There are few acceptable excuses for someone not replying or responding after a couple of days, and that's if he's a Physician on late shift duty, an emergency on hand, or surgeries. Since Physicians deal with life and death situations it's quite acceptable if he forgot to reply, having something else on his mind. A Pilot having had an oversees flight, is also a fair excuse; the long flight, plus the different time zones. And an emergency in the family, etc.

There's another trick <u>very smart men</u> play on women, to see all there is to see about the female of their interest. It's in actuality an old " Judges Trick", and very clever fellows, having come from Judicial families, or Lawyers of the old school, use that trick, too.

They're psychological tests, of sort, where he'll say something that sounds phonetically similar to another word ( homophones) to see what you heard, interpreted and how you react.

He'll say: I don't like juice......" which sounds as though the sentence is not finished, leaving a space for you to respond.

The possible spontaneous reaction will allow him a glimpse into the woman's mindset, such as:

" Are you an anti-Semite ?"

" You don't like Jewish people ?"

" Are you a Nazi ? "

" I don't either "

or,…

" Juice in general or specific juices ? "

" No", he says and explains, finishing the sentence, " I don't like juice
......with added coloring or with ' natural flavors'. If it's real orange
juice, why would it need added color or extra orange flavor ?"

Another phonetic trickery is:
" Do you know another word for Horse ?"

Her spontaneous reaction may be:
" Whores ? "

" Prostitute, Escort, Call Girl ? "

" Why would you ask me such a question ?

" What are you implying ?"

" Are you calling me a Whore ?" ( and he'll know right away she's
promiscuous )

To which he'll calmly say, while pretending to be somewhat taken
aback by what she understood:   " I wondered if there are other names
for horses. Cats are Felines. Cows are Cattle. Deers are game. What
are horses ?

And of course:

" Did you ever have to deal with lice ?"

Reactions:

" I can't stand it when people lie to me"

" What are you saying ? You think i'm lying to you ?"

" Have i ? Sure have, i could write books about it "

" My old boyfriend lied to me all the time ( and then she goes into the whole story revealing some baggage )

" Luckily no, but our dog had fleas once."

If the girl has ever caught bugs in certain areas, she'll turn red, feeling embarrassed.

Since STDs have been on the rise with Syphilis back, as well, after it was extinct in the western world for more than 50 years,  a lot of guys are more careful than ever and the smart ones know how to ask questions, from which we women can also learn a thing or two, to protect our health and well being.

Regardless how trendy it is, nowadays, for women ( and men) to shave themselves totally clean in the pubic area, looking prepubescent - many men ( and women ) know it's often done to cover up that they've contracted Syphilis at some point, which leaves small bald-circles.

Thus many men won't even take the chance to be intimate with a woman who's clean shaven. Though antibiotics treat the infection, many men ( and women) fear that the person may've become a ' carrier', able to infect them, while they're no longer infected.

In this high-alert time of Syphilis, most genuine men still appreciate ' fur', with the ' fur' comforting their possible fears. Aside from that, most healthy men, no matter what you may have been told, do not like it when women are clean shaven, because it looks <u>prepubescent</u> to them. They like women, adult women, and healthy adult women have pubic hair.

Another trick question is: " Did you ever have crabs ?"

If she's never had crabs, or any other STD she will most likely understand Crabs, as in Crustacean. If she contracted crabs in the past, or an STD, she will most likely project embarrassment; and even if she doesn't tell him the truth, he'll know by her reaction.

And then there's the little game playing, which is similar to THE GAME, but not to play ' reject' rather to get a glimpse into her personality.

Example:
You've been dating for a week, all is well. He sends a text, an email and you reply. But he's not replying. You inquire if he got your reply, but no answer. Since you've thus far had a good time casually dating, you automatically project everything that may worry you. If you're naturally concerned about everyone's well being, not taking anything personal, you inquire if everything is alright, assuring yourself he's well.

If you're vain and your ego gets in the way, you're not taking different possibilities into consideration; his well being, or that he may have lost his cell phone, or it fell into the bath tub, etc. thus you feel rejected ( taking it personal ) and tell him how rude he is, and so on.

In the meantime he's just observing how you'll react, what you'll say, what <u>words</u> you'll choose ; will you stay rational and well mannered ? Are you a sensible gal, or are you actually harsh ? Will you get angry, perhaps even vulgar ? How angry will you get ? Or are you being funny about his non-reactions ? By the way you'll react he'll see with what kind of a human being he's dealing.

# I'm no Pacifist.......
## i fight for Peace

Just know that if you're looking for a sensual man, he won't feel enticed to kiss lips of someone uttering 'gross' words like Sh..

But fair is fair, thus if you don't react for a day or two, just to see how he'll react, why not ? Sometimes it's not a bad idea to rock the boat a bit, to see with what kind of a ship you're dealing ; a ship that has integrity and is steadfast, with which to sail through a storm, or one that falls apart after a light blow of wind.

But, the possible Mr. Right Guy does not play The Game and calls you the next day to make plans for the weekend, asking if you'd like to go to a movie. If he already has a movie in mind, let's see if it's a genre you enjoy, and what his movie choice says about him.

If he suggests an A-typical guy flick - a car-chase movie - unless you're into cars - it's not a thoughtful choice; unless you shared how nuts you're about cars, car racing, etc.

If he were to say that he's planing to go see that Car Chase movie on saturday, asking if you'd like to come along, but you're not into that genre - be fair and let him know.

To compromise and watch a movie you wouldn't enjoy, just because you want to go out with him, is not fair to either of you. He won't have a good time enjoying the movie , if you're not enjoying it.

People often times discuss a movie afterward; what will you talk about ? How you didn't really care for the movie  ?

He'll have a much better time watching the movie alone or with a male friend. Generosity of spirit goes a long way. For all ye know he made plans to see that movie long before you two met, but was nice enough to ask if you want to come along.

If it's not your kind of entertainment, just tell him, he'll appreciate it.

Is he someone who likes Horror flicks - Dracula or Zombie movies ? If you're both into scary genres to feel the adrenaline rushing through your veins,( and OMG hold me tight ) have a ball, enjoy ' GLOOM - THE END is COMING ', or whatever these features are called.

Chances are your hair is dyed as jet-black as his hair, to fit the latest fashion trend of the NEW GOTHICs , along with pierced every things and the Skull, Dracula and bleeding Cross tattoos on most every part of your body.

If you're into this Gothic trend, you'll have some great pleasuring moments kissing and licking his metal piercings on lips, cheeks and what not, while caressing the monster tattoo on his chest.

Any man who likes animated movies, however - be it Disney's retellings of Grimm fairy tales, Beauty and the Beast, or original new animation a la Pixar, Dream Works, etc. - is open minded in so many ways, you can discuss just about every topic with him.

It's someone who's playful and can delight in the simple joys of life, as well. He's into thought provoking dramas, refined and brilliant suspense ( the Sixth Sense, the Spanish Prisoner, Gattaca ) clever comedies and romance epics with great twists. A man who enjoys animated movies may be many things, but one thing he is not; he's not pretentious.

Men, on the other hand, asserting that animated movies are kids-stuff, immature and childish, have an old attitude always trying to act oh so mature and grown-up, as well as pseudo-intellectual = pretentious.

Those are fellows who'll mention Plato's Republic or Dostoevsky while you're watching Wall-E, to try and sound smart while they've never actually taken as much as a peek into a classic work, but..... heard about it, and believe that dropping such names makes them look like Einstein.

A great idea for one of the first dates is to look at paintings, to get a glimpse into his mindset. One doesn't even have to go to a museum and can visit museums or galleries online - look at different paintings together, expressing curiosity what he sees in art. It's an incredible tool for mind reading, poetically speaking.

What and how much a person sees in abstract art reveals how much imagination someone has. The more imagination, the more he'll see in an abstract piece of art - entire stories can unfold.

A black canvas with but one small white circle can be seen as a night sky during full moon.

A melancholic person may see the overwhelming darkness, representing evil, overpowering the light, representing goodness.

Yet another person may believe it to mean, " The light at the end of the tunnel ", while someone else interprets it with even more optimism: " There's always a light, regardless how dark it is. "

Of course art is not for everyone, especially abstract art; but sharing what we perceive about a painting is the first step toward trust - to trust the other with one's inner most thoughts when observing the different shapes, colors, soft hues, roundness, stripes, squares or waves in a painting.

The most fascinating thing about art, in general, is that it will give us a glimpse into our own being when we allow art to 'speak' to us; allow it to touch our emotions, leading to self-discovery - acknowledging something we've not been consciously aware of.

When observing a painting that's overwhelming to you, due to too much chaos of colors and shapes, which may have a stressful effect on you, feel how exactly it effects you;

Does it hurt in your gut ?

Does it give you anxiety ?

Do you have to strain your eyes to even look at it ?

Is it the disorder that displeases you because you like order, or does it effect you as something being out of control, you're unable to control, thus would avoid looking at the painting ?

How does he feel about that painting ?

Now let's assume you share with him how the painting effected you ?

Will he say: " So, don't look at it. Let's look at another painting".

Or, will he talk down at you, telling you you're silly to be so effected by a painting ?

Or, will he be able to comfort you by relating a beautiful story he sees in that piece of art, taking away all of your initial anxiety about the painting, in which you're now seeing a charming tale ?

Sometimes we can't run away from problems in life and have to face them.

A great relationship is like the use of our two hands, left and right hand working <u>together</u> and doing so the two hands can lift a heavy item off the ground.

# Leaving some Mystery

Assuming you like the possible Mr. Right Guy a lot and he turns out to really care for you, too. You've been dating for 2 weeks, went to see a movie, you took some walks together through the park and through the city, noticing what window fronts he stopped at, thus what his other interests are - possibly a surprise visit to a music store - who woulda thunk the big guy plays the Piccolo ?

You'll discover something new about him every time you see him. Men usually reveal far less about themselves than women, unless they're eager to impress and you won't get a word in, but generally they know to keep some mystery.

Women, on the other hand, have the tendency ( in general) to talk a lot more, revealing too much of what he wants to uncover himself in time.

The low-cut dress, with but the nipples covered, leaving hardly anything to the imagination, may well have a sexually seductive effect on him, but when that's over with, what's to look forward to ? He won't even have to think of ideas to seduce her,  thus it will stop his creativity.

Let's hypothetically assume the fellow is musical, plays the guitar, piano, perhaps composes, writes songs. While he's enchanted and magnetically attracted, the fire of passion burning in his veins and that desires causes him of wanting to express what he feels;  he composes and writes the most heartfelt and original songs.

As long as he can still imagine what it would be like, he'll be creative and his songs will express his craving desire.

He'll see all in you his imagination has to offer - all of what is perfect to him, and the more you'll take your time, the more beautiful you'll become to him, because of how much more he's able to imagine. Once he had sex, the cat is out of the sack, and there's not much else left to..... imagine.

One of the reasons why people succeed in having long lasting relationships is because the woman mastered the art of keeping some mystery, keeping him enticed even after the couple has been intimate many times over.

Not to have sex in the first weeks ( or first few months) of dating, doesn't mean there shouldn't be any intimacy ; to hold each other, caress, hug and yes kiss each other is important, i would think ?

The kissing part, especially, is a precise tell-all of how sensual a man is - how compatible a couple is - and if they even enjoy kissing the other.

When a person doesn't want to kiss the other nor come close to his/ her lips, it's sometimes due to tight-hard lips, being unrelaxed, etc. but more often it's due to bad breath. Truly startling is when one never tells the other what the problem is. The man asks: " Is there a reason why you avoid kissing me ? "

To which she says :" Not at all ", then inhales deeply, holding her breath as if going for a deep sea dive, kisses him, steps back and .... exhales, taking another deep breath.

Both genders can fall victim to bad breath, and it's by far the biggest turn-off.

A lot of times it's due to what people are eating and the odor is a digestive odor from the stomach. No matter how often people with mouth-odor may brush their teeth, rinse with mouth-wash, or chew and suck on mints, it won't go away, unless they change their diet, after a thorough detox involving some activated charcoal to draw out the toxins.

High fat diets involving heartburn cause bad breath due to increased stomach acid. ( As does Bulimia with self-induced purging, due to stomach acid). Diets involving pork as a primary meat source cause bad breath as well.

But when both in a relationship share the same diet, they won't be effected by a specific smell emanating from the mouth or body, because they can't smell it since they share the same diet.

Someone who never eats pork, however, will smell this very specific odor right away, and will have a difficult time coming close to the person. Sharing a similar taste, and diet, is, as mentioned before, very important to having a sensual relationship.

No doubt Garlic can be the worst, and if you like garlic, as do i, chew some fresh parsley or mince some parsley and mix it with sesame oil, after you ate garlic; it will neutralize the odor.

Another reason for bad breath is of course flossing, or rather the lack thereof, with meat stuck between the teeth for who knows how long.

And of course tooth crowns, which need be throughly cleaned otherwise they'll give off a terrible metallic odor; not to forget bridges. Prosthetic bridges that can be removed and throughly cleaned every day, should be easy to take care of, but really bad can be built in bridges which aren't cleaned daily and thoroughly.

A blunder, in my opinion, is to use mouth-wash that has alcohol in it. It doesn't end up smelling fresh and minty, rather like hang-over breath. Many times i've suspected alcohol breath coming from someone, which turned out to be caused by Listerine.

If the man of your liking happens to have bad breath and it's not due to heartburn, nor a diet that's incompatible with yours, rather coming from his teeth, the problem can be easily solved by suggesting regular flossing ( if he has otherwise good teeth), occasionally brushing the teeth with baking soda - not Arm & Hammer, though; that's great for cleaning the bathtub, sink, and soaking ones feet if suffering from foot odor etc, but too harsh for the teeth.

I recommend baking soda that's used for ' baking', because it's much finer. A spoon full in warm water is also a great mouth rinse that neutralizes any odors. Another fabulous mouth rinse is cooled down licorice root tea, you can also drink. No sugar added, and it will give you the most deliciously sweet smelling breath, plus it's naturally anti-bacterial, eradicating odor causing bacteria on the tongue.

That just on a side note, because the majority of complaints from males and females about someone they were initially attracted to, is bad breath.

Now let's get back to leaving a little mystery, from which both partners benefit a whole lot. It creates a magic you'll never experience otherwise; that's the time when real magic happens - when in love and not extinguishing that flame before it gets really bright.

Being in-like, whatever one's aspirations, it brings out the 'muse' - the genie empowering a person to do things never thought possible, but suddenly there it is, that heavenly feeling making us glow, making us feel like.....flying.

Remember the Song ? " *I believe i can fly - i believe i can touch the sky* ".

Or, " *I got the world on a string, sitting on a rainbow, got the world around my finger, ...*"

The Beatles, too, shared the secret: " All you need is Love - Love is all you need".

I'll let you in on a little secret: Fairytales are metaphorically/allegorically revealed secrets. Perhaps you're familiar with Aladdin and the Wonder lamp. The Wonder lamp was not literally an oil lamp. An <u>Oil Lamp</u> is an allegory for a woman in love; a woman who is sincerely enticed by a man, thus 'glows' due to being a fertile oil-tree, so to speak.

This oil-lamp, this of honey dripping glowing creature in love, awakens the Genie inside the man, with him able to do anything he'll put his mind to during that time when so incredibly enticed by craving desire for her.

The flame that's enkindled inside him needs to burn fiercely and shine as brightly as it possibly can, and a woman's responsibility is to assure that flame will stay ablaze. If that fire is extinguished too early, he'll never experience his whole potential; thus a woman does him ( and herself) basically a favor when not saying yes, too quickly.

# Allow Virtue to exist.......
## without questioning its motives

# Epitaph

An Epi-taph is a last thought engraved into stone
A harmonious relationship is only possible when both are already
happy - doing what they like to do, pursuing a dream, working on
something they're passionate about and are just looking to share their
happiness, their contentment, with someone.
To look for someone to make you happy puts a lot of pressure on the
partner. What is he supposed to do, exactly, to make you happy ?

Made in the USA
Charleston, SC
06 October 2015